access to religion and philosophy

trp

Philosophy of Religion THIRD EDITION

Peter Cole

HODDER
EDUCATION
AN HACHETTE UK COMPANY

The Publishers would like to thank the following for permission to reproduce copyright material:

Photo credits

Cover © Design Pics/Imagestate; **p.24** © Mary Evans Picture Library; **p.35** © National Gallery Collection; By kind permission of the Trustees of the National Gallery, London/Corbis; **p.39** © ESA/Hubble Collaboration/Handout/CNP/Corbis; **p.80** © Jon Arnold Images Ltd/Alamy; **p.118** Richard H. Smith/Science Photo Library; **p.134** © Visual Arts Library (London)/Alamy.

Acknowledgements

p.8 Office of Public Sector Information (OPSI) for the quote from 'Unborn Children (Protection) Bill', *Parliamentary Debates* (*Hansard*) Volume 73, No. 62, 15 February 1985.

Every effort has been made to trace all copyright holders, but if any have been inadvertently overlooked the Publishers will be pleased to make the necessary arrangements at the first opportunity.

Hachette's policy is to use papers that are natural, renewable and recyclable products and made from wood grown in sustainable forests. The logging and manufacturing processes are expected to conform to the environmental regulations of the country of origin.

Orders: please contact Bookpoint Ltd, 130 Milton Park, Abingdon, Oxon OX14 4SB. Telephone: +44 (0)1235 827720. Fax: +44 (0)1235 400454. Lines are open 9.00a.m.–5.00p.m., Monday to Saturday, with a 24-hour message answering service. Visit our website at www.hoddereducation.co.uk

© Peter Cole 1999, 2004, 2008

First edition published 1999
Second edition published 2004

This third edition first published in 2008
by Hodder Education,
an Hachette UK Company
338 Euston Road
London NW1 3BH

Impression number   5 4 3

Year   2012 2011

Illustrations by GreenGate Publishing
Typeset in Bembo by GreenGate Publishing Services, Tonbridge, Kent
Printed in India

A catalogue record for this title is available from the British Library

ISBN: 978 0 340 95778 3

Philosophy of Religion THIRD EDITION

CONTENTS

PREFACE

To the student

Access books are written mainly for students studying for examinations at higher level, particularly GCE Advanced Subsidiary (AS) level and Advanced (A) level. A number of features have been included to assist students, such as the study guides at the end of chapters.

To use these books most effectively, you should be aware of the following features:

- At the beginning of each chapter there is a checklist, which is a brief introduction about the key elements that the chapter covers.
- Key questions, words, people, thoughts and quotes in the margin highlight specific points from the main text.
- Profiles of key individuals give information on a philosopher's background and work.
- There are summary diagrams throughout the chapters to aid revision.
- The revision checklist at the end of each chapter summarises the main points.

General advice on answering essay questions

Structured questions will tell you what to include. The following advice is for those questions which leave it to you to work out.

- The most important thing is to read the question carefully and work out what it really means. Make sure you understand all the words in the question (you may need to check some of them in the dictionary or look up technical terms in the glossary at the back of this book).
- Gather the relevant information for answering the question. You will probably not need everything you know on the topic. Keep to what the question is asking.
- Organise your material by drawing up a plan of paragraphs. Make sure that each paragraph is relevant to the question. Include different views within your answer (most questions require arguments for and against).

- Start with an introduction that explains in your own words what the question is asking and defines any technical words. Work through your answer in carefully planned paragraphs. Write a brief conclusion in which you sum up your answer to the question (without repeating everything in the essay).

TOOLS FOR THE JOB

Chapter checklist ✓

This chapter examines what is meant by 'philosophy of religion' and considers some of the areas that would be studied in such a course. Philosophical arguments are discussed with particular reference to inductive and deductive arguments.

---

1 Studying philosophy

Key word

Philosophy: literally 'a love of wisdom'. The actual subject area is disputed and ranges from linguistic analysis to questions about ultimate reality.

Key quote

'Philosophy begins in wonder.'
PLATO

Key questions

What is the business of philosophy?

Why does philosophy seem to produce more problems than it solves?

According to the philosopher AJ Ayer, the business of **philosophy** is to clarify and analyse. To many students starting out on philosophy, such a view does not match their experiences. If anything, philosophy seems to make things more complex and confusing, and produce problems where none appeared before!

a) Challenges popular common sense and basic assumptions

There may be many explanations to account for this common experience, but I think part is due to the boldness of philosophy in challenging popular common sense and basic assumptions. Philosophy is not satisfied with the claim that 'it's obvious' or 'it's common sense'. Rather, it seeks to challenge the view that common sense = truth. It can challenge beliefs that you may hold very dear, and it never claims to provide answers to the ultimate questions. Students may often end up feeling they know less than before they started!

b) Challenge of technical language

Another difficulty experienced by students new to philosophy is the subject-specific language. Every subject study area faces this problem. However, it is important to use the right language and to do so from the start. It is essential to understand the exact meanings of technical words and to be comfortable using them. Many students try to side-step this task – a task that can be hard work – only to find themselves confused later because of some basic misunderstandings.

c) Challenge of close argument

A philosophy book is not usually light reading or something to read just before going to sleep at bedtime! Usually it is helpful to take notes and even to write out the arguments for yourself, so that you are clear about the path of reasoning. Because of the often close argument, you may well find yourself having to read a page two or three times over. This is quite normal and you should not take it as a sign of failure on your part to understand.

d) The benefits

You will find that the discipline that you develop by studying philosophy helps you in your other studies as well. It sharpens your mind to grapple with such things as the definitions of concepts. You will become more aware of what does and does not constitute a valid argument. You will also develop the skill of following and evaluating arguments. A further benefit is that such study gives insight into the history of ideas and the debates that have accompanied them. It will force you to examine your own ideas and presuppositions. As Socrates concluded: 'Life that is not examined is life that is not worth living.'

2 Philosophy of religion

The word 'philosophy' means literally 'love of wisdom'. As I have indicated, two of the concerns of philosophy are to clarify the meanings of words and to identify ways of testing for logical coherency. It is not a subject in its own right – it is always the philosophy *of* something, such as science, education or mind. In particular, the philosophy of religion examines the general philosophical problems about religion and God. It analyses concepts such as God and eternal life, tries to determine the meaning of religious utterances and examines the nature and existence of a God or gods and the way in which God is related to the world.

Although the contents of a philosophy of religion course can vary significantly, nonetheless it has always been the tradition to include an examination of the classical arguments for the existence of God. There are generally considered to be five classical arguments, although there are numerous other arguments for God. Four of the five are based on observable phenomena such as the order within the universe (**teleological** argument) or the

Key words

Theistic: belief in the existence of one divine reality, who is distinct from creation.

Natural theology: the use of reasoned argument to assess basic religious claims, such as the existence of God.

Revealed theology: claims about God derived from 'revelations' from special experiences of God or sacred writings.

experiences of many people of things beyond the natural order (religious experience). The fifth is based on the concept of God, from which it is argued that when the concept is properly understood, it will be seen that it must have a reality in existence. We will look at these in detail in the next chapter, but before discussing the **theistic** proofs (an attempt to prove by argument that God exists) we need some 'tools of the trade'. We need to understand what constitutes a good or a bad argument.

The very idea that we can reason out the arguments for God and be convinced about them is known as **natural theology**. This assumes that we can use our cognitive faculties to reach conclusions about whether God exists or not. In this approach, no special religious authority is appealed to. This contrasts with **revealed theology** where claims about God derive from 'revelations' from special experiences of God or sacred writings. Perhaps the distinction between the two is slightly blurred since arguments can be formulated for God's existence based on, for example, religious experience or miracles. Both of these arguments claim special experiences but both still require us to reason out whether God exists.

3 Philosophical arguments

a) What is a reasoned argument?

Key words

Argument: a set of statements which is such that one of them (the conclusion) is supported or implied by the others (the premises).

Valid argument: the correct logical structure of a deductive argument.

The philosophy of religion has concerned itself with reasoned arguments. However, what is an **argument**? What constitutes a proof?

An argument can be defined as 'a set of statements which is such that one of them (the conclusion) is supported or implied by the others (the premises)', for example:

- The Eiffel Tower is in Paris.
- Paris is in France.

Therefore the Eiffel Tower is in France.

The first two statements are the *premises*, and the third is the *conclusion*.

A **valid argument** is one where there are no mistakes in logic. Hence the above argument is a valid argument. However, beware: not all valid arguments are therefore true. For example, consider the following argument:

- The Eiffel Tower is in Worthing.
- Worthing is in England.

Therefore the Eiffel Tower is in England.

There is nothing wrong with the logic here! However, there seems plenty wrong in agreeing with the conclusion. The problem is, of course, that one of the premises is untrue. Hence even if the logic is impeccable, it does not mean to say that the conclusion is true. To acknowledge this problem, philosophy refers to an argument where both the logic is correct and the premises are true as a *sound argument*.

b) Deductive arguments

Key word

Proof: a sequence of steps that establishes the truth of a proposition.

Key question

What is philosophical proof?

Key word

Deductive argument: an argument whose structure dictates that if the premises are true, the conclusion must be true.

A sound argument is what we really mean by philosophical **proof**. To put it another way: a definition of proof is 'that which results from a valid argument constructed from a set of true premises'. To be compelling, the premises would have to be known to be true by those offering the proof and by those to whom it is offered. A proof is such that if you agree with the premises then you would have to agree with the conclusion. Indeed, to accept the premises and deny the conclusion would be self-contradictory. This type of argument is called **deductive argument**.

If philosophy only considered this type of argument then disputes between philosophers would be less numerous, and fewer philosophy books would be written. However, there is another type of argument that is less persuasive but more common.

c) Inductive arguments

Consider the following argument:

- If it rains, I shall get wet.
- I get wet.

Therefore it rained.

I could imagine an instance where, though I agreed with the premises, I did not agree with the conclusion. For instance, I did not get wet because it rained, but because a student crept up behind me and threw a bucket of water over me! In other words, there are more ways of getting wet than just by rain. To express it more formally: the conclusion does not necessarily follow from the premises. The premises provide some, but not absolute, support for the conclusion. Indeed, to accept the premises and deny the conclusion (as we have seen) would not be self-contradictory.

Key question

What is the difference between a deduction argument and an inductive argument?

Key word

Inductive argument: an argument whose structure dictates that even if the premises are true, the conclusion may not be true.

As we said, philosophers are concerned with clarity, so they distinguish between the two types of argument. We saw that the first type, which we called valid, is known as a *deductive argument*. This second type is called **inductive**. Unfortunately, this can often lead to confusion, particularly if you are an ardent fan of the detective Sherlock Holmes. Sherlock Holmes prided himself on his deductive reasoning. As far as philosophers are concerned, it was induction! To conclude that someone has a dog because they have dog hairs on their trousers is not deduction but induction. After all, they could have brushed against a dog just prior to calling in at 221B Baker

Street. Chapter 2 in Conan Doyle's *A Study in Scarlet* is entitled 'The science of deduction'. In this chapter Dr Watson lists the skills of Sherlock Holmes and accurately notes against his knowledge of philosophy: 'Nil!'

Remember that identifying the type of argument (that is, deciding it is deductive or inductive) does not, in itself, prove whether the conclusion is true or false. We must also decide whether the individual premises are true or false. Types of argument merely tell you about the logical connection between the premises and the conclusion.

The problem with inductive arguments is their obvious limitation of always being open to doubt and uncertainty. Equally, the problem with deductive arguments is that they are also limited. It is difficult to establish the original premises, and the conclusions reached are often obvious from the original premises. Indeed, by necessity the original premises must already contain the conclusion.

Key thought

Identifying the type of argument does not, in itself, prove whether the conclusion is true or false.

Figure 1 Deductive and inductive arguments

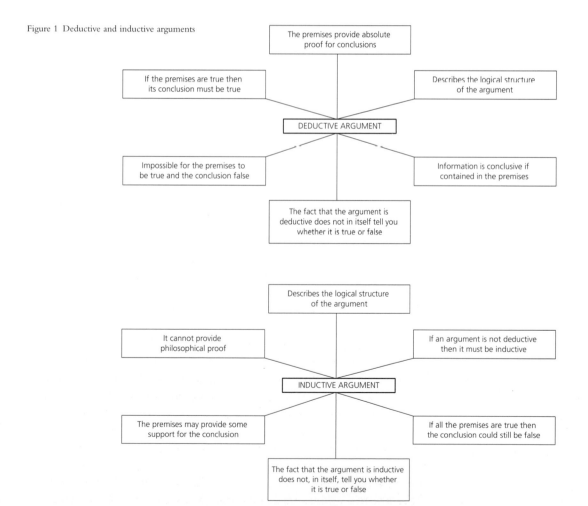

d) Assessing arguments

All this rather theoretical introduction to arguments may seem rather irrelevant. 'When are we going to get to the philosophy?' you ask. However, identifying the key premises of a complex argument is a vital task. Setting out arguments in a formal way with premises and conclusion is also important for clarity. Assessing arguments becomes much easier and a basic checklist can then be followed:

Key question

How are arguments assessed?

- Is each of the premises true?
- Is the argument valid (without logical error)?
- If inductive, how persuasive is it?

One problem is assessing 'levels of persuasiveness' of inductive arguments. Something that is convincing to one person often carries no weight with another. We need to be conscious of the various presuppositions that each of us holds, and how these affect the way we interpret the evidence. Also, we must acknowledge that different types of evidence are appropriate to the differing areas under investigation. For example, scientific evidence involves observation from which a hypothesis (a suggested explanation) is formed. This is then tested by a series of experiments. If the expected results from the experiments do not occur, a modified hypothesis has to be formulated, taking into account the new observations. However, if the expected results *do* occur, it does *not* mean that the hypothesis is finally proven, but rather that it has escaped disproof. Obviously the more times the hypothesis escapes disproof, the more certain one becomes of its truth.

Key question

What is the difference between scientific evidence and historical evidence?

In contrast, historical evidence involves assessing such things as documents, artefacts and circumstantial evidence, as well as interpreting that evidence. The conclusion reached will be on the scale of different degrees of certainty – certain, probable, possible, improbable, impossible.

Even the scientific method has become modest in its claims of proof. Scientific laws are increasingly seen as descriptions of what we expect to happen, rather than what must happen. Indeed, some would argue that nothing can be *proved* by experimental means since an infinite number of tests would be required. For instance, every time we heat iron, it expands. But what about the iron we have not heated? How can we be certain that iron will expand? To be certain we would have to heat every piece of iron, and even then we could never be sure that it would expand next time we heated it.

Key question

Is proof possible?

Figure 2 Degree of premises' support for conclusion

Non-arguments	*Inductive arguments*	*Deductive arguments*
None	Weak	Absolute
	Reasonable	
	Strong	

Study guide

By the end of this chapter you should understand the difference between a deductive and an inductive argument, as well as the various connotations of the word 'proof'.

Revision checklist

Can you define each of the following words?

■ Inductive
■ Deductive
■ Argument
■ Proof
■ Theistic
■ Theology.

Do you know the difference between the following?

■ Inductive arguments–deductive arguments
■ Natural theology–revealed theology
■ Proof–probable
■ Valid–sound.

Do you know the basic checklist for assessing arguments?

Example of exam question

AO1

Knowledge and understanding assessment objective.

AO2

Evaluation assessment objective.

Read the following extract on abortion, from a debate in Parliament. Express the argument in terms of premises and a conclusion.

> MR ENOCH POWELL: *I beg to move, that the Bill be now read a second time. The Bill has a single and simple purpose. It is to render it unlawful for a human embryo created by* in vitro *[laboratory] fertilisation to be used as the subject of experiment or, indeed, in any other way or for any other purpose except to enable a woman to bear a child …*
>
> *It is argued … that to permit the use of a fertilised embryo for research would open the way to new and useful medical knowledge. I do not stand here as a layman to dispute that. True, I must admit I*

have a suspicion that the inquiring human spirit will, if denied one avenue of arriving at truth and information, speedily find other ways of doing so. I have also been impressed to find profound difference of opinion on this very point among people apparently equally qualified in the medical profession and in the sciences.

Nevertheless, I do not ask the House to reject the proposition. On the contrary, I ask the House to face it. I ask the House, in coming to a decision, to make the assumption that by means of what the Bill will prohibit, useful and beneficial knowledge would in future be obtained. I ask the House to exercise a choice – and to decide that nevertheless the moral, human and social cost of that information being obtained in a way that outrages the instincts of so many is too great a price to pay.

From 'Unborn Children (Protection) Bill', *Parliamentary Debates* (*Hansard*) Volume 73, No. 62, 15 February 1985.

2

Chapter checklist

This chapter looks at the nature of God by examining the key attributes of God. These attributes raise a number of philosophical problems such as whether they are coherent and consistent. These problems are then examined.

1 Introduction

Key words

Theism: the belief in the existence of God transcendent – having existence outside the universe.

Materialism: the view that the material universe is all that exists.

Theism and **materialism** are two very different views of reality. Theism is the belief that reality is made up of God Himself and all that God creates. In contrast, materialism claims that only the physical world exists and so denies the existence of God. Philosophy seeks to investigate reality by means of reason and by weighing up evidence, concerned at all times that propositions are coherent and consistent. However, the very concept of God, at the centre of theism, raises a number of difficulties.

2 Terminology

Key words

Atheism: a belief that there is no God.

Deism: the view that God created the universe but is now not directly involved in creation.

Agnostic: a person who does not believe it is possible to know whether God exists.

According to A Thiselton (*A Concise Encyclopedia of the Philosophy of Religion*, 2002), the term 'theism' emerged in the seventeenth century to denote belief in God, in contrast to both **atheism** and **deism**. Atheism is the belief that there is no God and so the world is all there is. In contrast, the **agnostic** is someone who has suspended judgement about the existence of God. They are unable to decide one way or the other. Just as there is a clear difference between a theist and an atheist, so there is between a theist and a deist. A deist, like the classical theist, believes in one God who created and sustains the universe, but does not believe that God is actively involved with the world. This view sees God more of an observer than a participator. The involvement of God in miracles, for example, is not acceptable to a deist.

Key word

Pantheism: the idea that the whole universe is God or part of God.

One other term connected with the family of 'theisms' is **pantheism**, literally meaning that God is everything. It does not see God as creator and separate from the universe He made. Indeed the universe is God and so has always existed. Although pantheism may sound similar to atheism in its belief about reality, it is in the family of 'theisms' because it argues that the universe has goals that it is pursuing. The universe is purposeful and intelligent and has direction.

3 The key attributes of God

Key thought

We need to define the kind of being we are talking about before we can go on to enquire whether such a being exists.

Key question

What is the definition of God?

Key quotes

'God is that than which nothing greater can be conceived.'
ANSELM

'God is a supremely perfect being.'
DESCARTES

It could be argued that it makes more sense to find out whether God exists before worrying about what God is like. However, when we are discussing the existence of God, what we are doing is asking whether there is any evidence that a particular kind of being exists. Hence the examination of the attributes of such a being will help clarify our arguments about its possible existence. At this stage no assumption is being made about its existence. When we have defined the kind of being we are talking about, we then go on to enquire whether any such being exists.

It is appropriate at this point to see how some philosophers have sought to define this being. Anselm defined God as 'that than which nothing greater can be conceived' (see chapter 3). By this he meant that God was the greatest possible being, the one who maximised all possible qualities. Nothing could be superior or even equal to God, since to be equal with God would mean that God was not the greatest. Descartes developed this approach in his argument for God and defined God as 'a supremely perfect being'. (It should be noted that this approach to God is using the Christian tradition though it is applicable to other monotheistic faiths. For a survey of other views of God, see chapter 3 in R Solomon's *The Big Questions*, 1998.)

Starting from such a definition of God as 'a perfect being' may seem reasonable as it incorporates the idea of an object worthy of worship. However, the problem arises as to what are the exact attributes that a perfect being would possess. Various philosophers have attempted to list the possible attributes. For instance, HP Owen (*Concepts of Deity*, 1971), R Swinburne (*The Coherence of Theism*, 1977) and R Nash (*The Concept of God*, 1983) all identify various attributes of the nature of God associated with the classical monotheistic traditions. The key ones are:

Key word

Ex nihilo: Latin phrase meaning 'out of nothing', that is, God did not use any previously existing materials when He created.

- Creator – God is creator of all things other than Himself. He created the universe out of nothing ('*ex nihilo*') and gives it purpose. God is separate from His creation.

Key words

Transcendent: God is greater than and distinct from his creation.

Immanence: God's involvement in his creation.

Incorporeal: without material form.

Omnipotent: God is able to do all His holy will.

- Sustainer – the created things are totally dependent on God for their existence from moment to moment. Without God, the universe would collapse into nothingness.
- Personal – a basic concept of a religious life is that God can enter into relationships with people. He also performs actions.
- **Transcendent** – often expressed as God's 'otherness'. God is unique and distinct from creation. He has existence outside the created world. Balanced against this is God's **immanence**, denoting God's presence and action within the world.
- Self-existent – God depends on nothing other than Himself.
- Eternal – this has two aspects. One has to do with duration, in that God is seen as always existing by nature rather than choice. He cannot choose to cease to exist. He is everlasting. The second aspect focuses on God's timelessness.
- **Incorporeal** – God is not a material thing. God does not occupy space to the exclusion of other things. He is not body but spirit.
- **Omnipotent** – God can do everything that is logically possible. Some, like Descartes, argue that God can also do the logically impossible. Others restrict God's power further by arguing that God can only perform acts that are consistent with His own nature (for example, in 2 Timothy 2:13 St Paul claims that 'God cannot deny Himself').
- **Omniscient** – this is often regarded as a subset of omnipotence. God knows all things and never believes anything that is false. Some would want to restrict that knowing to only those things that are possible to know.
- Omnipresent – God is not limited by either space or time.
- All loving – God is love.
- Perfectly good – God is morally perfect.

4 Are the attributes self-consistent?

Key question

Do the attributes of God lead to contradiction and incoherency?

For the concept of God to have meaning, the attributes proposed must be self-consistent and consistent with one another. A lack of self-consistency would mean that the concept was incoherent and therefore meaningless. It might be argued that we cannot know what God is like, as God is transcendent. Even if that is true and God can only be known by revelation, what we believe about God still has to make sense to us. If what is believed is not understood or doesn't make sense, then it is hard to see how there is any content to the belief.

Philosophers have challenged several of the attributes outlined above on the grounds that the concept is **contradictory** or **incoherent**.

Key question

What does it mean to say 'God is timeless'?

a) Eternal

The idea of God being timeless is a concept that has taxed many a philosopher. The classical view argued for by philosophers such as Augustine, Anselm and Aquinas sees God as outside of time. God sees all things as eternally present. Aquinas used the illustration of someone sitting on a hill watching people walking below. The view of the walkers is that of people in front, beside and behind them; in other words a particular spatial order. However, the observer on the hill is outside of that spatial order yet observes all the order in one view. Similarly God could see all time in one view. Another illustration Aquinas used was of a circle where the centre point represents eternity and the circumference represents time. Likewise Augustine took the view that the author of the space–time continuum could not be bound by it.

More recent support for this view of God outside of time has come from the theory of special relativity. K Rogers (*Perfect Being Theology*, 2000) explains:

> *If time is relative to particular observational frameworks, then there is no absolute, universal time which would encompass God and the physical world. (p. 56)*

Key question

Can God be outside of time?

However, many regard such a concept of God outside of time as self-contradictory or incoherent. It is argued that the theory of special relativity actually argues for an absolute and universal time for the entire physical universe. There is still a lively debate among physicists about the nature of time, or even whether it exists. It would be unwise to be dogmatic on this issue.

More traditional rejections of God outside of time involve the claim that our thoughts and desires are all performed in the present with reference to the past and future, and they take time. However, the claim of timelessness for God demands that all of God's actions and thoughts and desires take place simultaneously. There is only the 'now' for a God who is timeless. Such things as remembering or acting seem impossible for a God who is timeless. How could God act in particular events in history such as the parting of the Red Sea, since it would seem to require Him to enter a time frame? In particular, the creation of a universe is problematic if there is no time frame in God Himself – for there has to be a time when God decides to bring the universe into being and a time when there was no universe. In other words, it is not at all clear what it means to say that God acts 'timelessly' in time. For the Christian, the issue is particularly problematic since it makes the claim that God became man and entered human history. Swinburne (*Is There a God?*, 1996) concludes:

Key question

What does it mean to say 'God acts timelessly in time'?

> *I prefer the understanding of God being eternal as His being everlasting rather than as His being timeless. (p. 9)*

However, to claim that God is bounded by time also gives rise to charges of incoherency. If God exists in time, then His past and future would limit His present.

b) Omnipotent

Philosophers do not generally regard the idea that God cannot do the logically impossible, or perform acts that are inconsistent with His nature, as a limitation of His power. Hence it is argued that God cannot make square circles and God cannot sin. In a sense, God not doing the logically impossible can be seen as a reflection of His nature, since it would require Him to do something contrary to reason.

However, many argue that omnipotence is self-contradictory. The classic attacks on this concept have been expressed by means of paradoxes:

- The paradox of the stone shows there are things God cannot do. The paradox is stated in the question 'Can God create a stone that He cannot lift?' If He can create the stone, then He lacks power to lift it, but if He cannot create such a stone, then He also lacks power. Various attempts have been made to find a solution to remove the apparent contradiction. The most favoured response points out that it is a logical impossibility for God to create a stone He cannot lift, since He is all-powerful. Hence it does not detract from His omnipotence.
- Another paradox is whether God can create a creature whose will is so free that God cannot control it. One resolution to this problem is to argue that it is logically impossible for a choice to be both free and controlled at the same time.
- Another paradox is whether God has the power to change the past. The implication is that the past cannot be changed and therefore God is not all-powerful. Once again the appeal to logical impossibilities resounds. If the past is changed, then it ceases to be the past.

It could also be questioned whether omnipotence is a necessary attribute of God. God may choose to limit His divine power in the interests of love, but in that case He does remain all-powerful, unless He cedes His power permanently.

c) Omniscient

Omniscience is the ability to know everything. Philosophers point out a possible incoherency if it is also claimed that God makes decisions. God can't know His own decisions while He is making them, yet if God is omniscient, He would know all things including those decisions. This seems a contradiction. One solution is to say that God makes those decisions outside of time. In other words, as God is timeless, He sees the past, present and future, all in the same moment.

d) Omnipresent

Omnipresence should not be confused with the idea of 'God in everything', which is more akin to pantheism. But if God is a person, how can He be everywhere? Aquinas resolved this dilemma by stating that God's presence 'everywhere' meant there was unlimited scope for God's operative powers. In other words, God affects everything. This shows how important it is to define terms. Clear definition may help remove apparent contradictions.

e) All-loving

It is difficult to define a state of 'all-loving'. Some philosophers argue that love has no limits. This is expressed by the phrase 'love has no intrinsic maximum' (see ontological argument, p. 21).

f) Perfectly good

Perhaps a stronger problem revolves around the question of the relation between goodness and God. What is the source of the standard of moral goodness? Is God the source of moral goodness, or is there a standard of goodness to which God is subject to conform? This dilemma is not new and can be found in Plato's *Euthyphro*. Put simply, does good exist independently and separate from approval, or does good exist as a consequence of it being approved?

Either answer creates a problem. If God commands things because they are good, then it implies there is a standard of goodness independent of God. In this case, God is no longer the creator of everything. There is a standard of values outside of his control and creativity. However, the alternative is no less problematic. If whatever God thinks and does is simply by definition 'good', regardless of what it is, then does it make sense to praise God for his goodness?

One possible solution is to accept that there is an objective standard but the standard is not external to God, but internal. Morality is grounded in the character of God, who is perfectly good. His commands are rooted in His character. That is not the same thing as saying that God and good are identical. God is not *the very same thing* as goodness. Goodness is an essential characteristic of God.

5 Are the attributes consistent with one another?

Besides the need for self-consistency for the attributes of God, there is also a requirement that the attributes are consistent with one another.

Key question

Are there things God cannot know?

Key question

Can God be everywhere at the same time?

Key question

Does God command things because they are good, or are things good because God commands them?

Key quotes

'We can think of God Himself, the individual being, as the supreme standard of goodness.'
WILLIAM ALSTON

'Morality is not grounded ultimately in God's commands, but in His character, which then expresses itself in his commands.'
SCOTT RAE, *MORAL CHOICES – AN INTRODUCTION TO ETHICS*

a) Omnipotent, omniscient, creator and perfectly good

These four attributes of God would seemingly make the existence of evil an impossibility. (For a full discussion of this issue see chapter 11.)

b) Eternal, omniscient and free/responsible

Key question

Can God know the future?

How can God know the future, since it has not yet been decided? The concept is full of difficulties. If God does know the future, some would argue it implies there are no acts of free will, since He knows what will happen. Alternatively, if God doesn't know the future, then He is not omniscient. Others argue that the fact that God knows the future doesn't therefore necessitate Him over-riding my free will. He merely knows what free choice I make. Though I am in time, God is outside of time. A famous attempt at a solution was proposed by Luis de Molina (1536–1600). Molina maintained that God would know what people would freely choose to do in all circumstances where some choice was available. This included choices that were hypothetical in that either the person or the circumstances never came into being. Such knowledge was termed **middle knowledge**.

Key people

Luis de Molina (1536–1600) was a Jesuit who attempted to reconcile predestination and free will.

In contrast, Swinburne rejects the view of God as outside of time and argues that God only knows that which it is logically possible to know. This then excludes events that God permits that are the result of free will choices by humans. Such events God would not know, but supporters of this view do not regard it as a loss of omniscience.

Key word

Middle knowledge: God knows what every creature would do in any given set of circumstances, even if those circumstances never actually occur.

Certainly the problem has been recognised for centuries and a good discussion can be found in G Hughes' article 'Omniscience', in B Davies (ed.), *Philosophy of Religion: A Guide to the Subject* (1998), pp. 86–94.

Figure 3 Nature of God

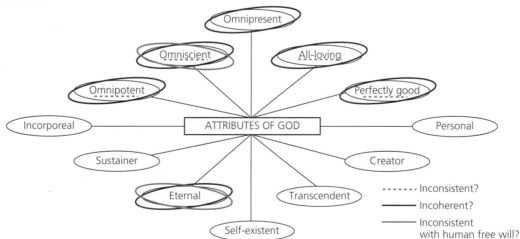

6 Recent developments

Key people

Don Cupitt (b 1934)
is a Fellow of Emmanuel College, Cambridge. A populariser of the view that sees true religion in terms of joy in life and an active attempt to add value to the human lifeworld.

Key quote

'... God is a symbol that represents to us everything that spirituality requires of us and promises of us.'

DON CUPITT

In recent times there has been a challenge to the traditional debate about the concept of God. Theologians like Don Cupitt have questioned the whole notion of God as a real, external, objective being. Cupitt argues that God is just a symbol for the religious and spiritual life. In his book *Taking Leave of God* (1980), Cupitt states:

> *I do not suppose God to be an objectified individual over and above the religious requirement. (p. 85)*

Indeed Cupitt offers a new definition of 'God'. In this new way of understanding religion,

> *God is Christian spirituality in coded form, for God is a symbol that represents to us everything that spirituality requires of us and promises to us. (p. 14)*

Modern linguistic philosophy has tended to insist that we need to define our terms first, before investigating their place in the real world. We can define God in any way we like, but we are not having a meaningful debate unless those in dispute have an agreed definition of the being whose existence they are considering. In other words, we can only debate the existence of God if we have an agreed definition of God. In a similar way we can only debate the issue of whether the moon is made of green cheese if we have an agreed understanding of what we mean by the moon. Otherwise debate is literally meaningless.

Cupitt's definition of God would mean that the traditional concepts of God would be understood in a very different way. Omnipotence, for example, would:

> *not refer to the power of a creator God, but to the power inherent in each one of us if we would give up living for ourselves and instead devote ourselves to others. (P Vardy, The Puzzle of God [1990], p. 120)*

Study guide

By the end of this chapter you should know and understand the key terms connected with theism as well as the main attributes of God. You should also be aware of the possible philosophical conflicts between those attributes and be able to discuss issues about their coherency and consistency.

Revision checklist

Can you define each of the following words?

- Theism
- Pantheism
- Transcendent
- Omniscience
- Omnipresence.

Do you know the difference between the following?

- Theism–deism
- Agnosticism–atheism
- Omnipotence–omniscience
- Transcendence–immanence
- Creator–sustainer.

Can you explain why the following are seen by some to be incoherent/inconsistent?

- God's omnipotence
- God is perfectly good
- God's omniscience and human free will.

Examples of exam questions

1 Identify and briefly describe two of God's properties.

There are two trigger words that need to be addressed. Candidates would be expected to identify appropriate attributes and also provide an accurate description of what each attribute entails. Lower level answers would be where candidates only identified and described one property fully or identified both properties but did not go on to describe those properties in any depth.

It is important to select two properties that you can say more about than just their definition.

2 Explain the philosophical problems that arise when combining two or more of God's properties.

This is what is called an AO1 skill question because what is being asked for is knowledge and understanding. However, many candidates may well misread this as an evaluative skill (AO2) question and engage in a detailed critical assessment. However, the question does not actually ask candidates to resolve the problems, merely to identify them.

Again it is important to select properties where there is something of substance to explain.

Further question to consider

To what extent does the attribute of God's omniscience raise philosophical problems?

Chapter checklist ✓

This chapter covers the classical forms of the ontological argument for the existence of God by Anselm and Descartes. Two modern forms by Malcolm and Plantinga are also discussed. The arguments are then evaluated in respect of their strengths and weaknesses and the extent to which they can be considered a proof for God.

1 The classic arguments for the existence of God

a) A priori and a posteriori

As we saw in chapter 1 (p. 5), identifying the type of argument (that is, deciding if it is deductive or inductive) does not, in itself, prove whether the conclusion is true or false. We must also decide whether the individual premises are true or false. Types of argument merely tell you about the logical connection between the premises and the conclusion. How then do we decide about the truth value of the premises?

Consider the following premise:

- Charles gains a grade A at AS Religious Studies.

How do I go about finding out if that is true? I would have to go and check it out in some way – maybe look at a list of published results or ask to see Charles' certificate from the exam board. I cannot assume that Charles has a grade A at AS Religious Studies. I would need to make some kind of investigation. I could only conclude the truth value in the light of some experience (for example, seeing the certificate). If this is the case then the premise is said to be **a posteriori** (after experience).

Some premises may be such that their truth value can be decided without reference to experience. Consider the following premise:

- The circle is square.

Key question ?

How do we decide the truth value of a premise?

Key word

A posteriori: from or after experience.

Key word

A priori: prior to experience.

I do not need to investigate the truth of whether a circle is square. I know that the premise is false. By definition a circle is round not square. Premises such as these are called **a priori**, meaning that their truth value can be determined without reference to any experience (that is, any investigation).

The classical arguments for God's existence comprise of arguments of which only one, the ontological argument, has a priori premises. All the other arguments have a posteriori premises.

b) What are the main classical arguments?

There are five classical, theistic proofs. Four of them attempt to demonstrate the existence of God from some observation or experience of the universe. These are:

Key thought

Deductive arguments offer proof whilst inductive arguments only offer probabilities.

- The cosmological argument, which infers God from the existence of the world or from phenomena within it, such as causality.
- The teleological argument, which infers a designer from the occurrence of order and regularity in the world.
- The moral argument, which infers God as the explanation for moral consciousness or the guarantor for the highest good.
- The religious experience argument, which sees God as the best explanation for experiences that people claim that are beyond the normal.

Key word

Empiricism: The view that the dominant foundation of knowledge is experience.

Because these all involve claims about the world that can be investigated **empirically** (by the senses) or verified by experience, they are a posteriori arguments. Thus they contain premises that are based on experience, such as order in the world or moral consciousness.

In contrast, the fifth argument is a priori. Such premises are prior to any experience of the world, and are not verified by experience. This argument for the existence of God is:

- The ontological argument, which concludes that God's definition entails His existence.

As we look at each of the arguments in turn, it will be clear that each comes in a variety of versions. I have selected the key versions, but in your supplementary reading you may well come across other approaches. Added to this is the problem that not all philosophers actually agree how to interpret the proofs, since their views about the meaning of the word 'God', for instance, will affect their interpretations. We will return to the issue of the value of the proofs after we have considered the individual theistic proofs.

Traditionally, the arguments have all been regarded as deductive and flawed. However, in more recent years the a posteriori arguments have been presented as inductive and are assessed in terms of persuasiveness. Swinburne, in particular, has taken this approach in his book *The Existence of God* (1979). The cumulative approach in considering all the arguments together as persuasive of God's existence is another trend of the last century.

We will consider first the one argument that has remained deductive in its form – the ontological argument.

Figure 4 Classic arguments for God

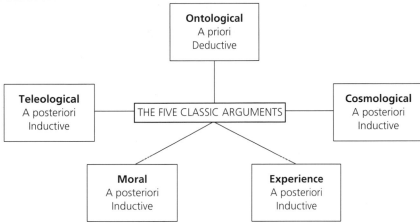

2 The ontological argument

a) Historical background

Ontological literally means 'concerned with being'. This argument was most classically propounded by Anselm (1033–1109). The actual argument can be found in chapters 2–4 of Anselm's *Proslogion* (1077–78). The argument was sharply criticised in his own time, and centuries later by such people as Aquinas and Immanuel Kant. Among those who have supported it are Descartes, and more recently Malcolm and Plantinga. This argument appeals more to those who already believe in God than to the atheist. Scholars seem divided as to whether Anselm meant the argument to be effective to the atheist.

As we have noted above, the argument differs from all other proofs in being a priori (prior to experience) since it proceeds from the idea of God – instead of arguing a posteriori (based on experience), that is, from some feature of the universe. As an a priori argument it has as its ground a logical demonstration that either totally succeeds or totally fails.

Its scope is greater than that of the other arguments since they can give only a limited view of what God is like, while the concept of God as 'the most perfect being' implies a whole range of other qualities.

b) Anselm's argument

i) First form

Anselm began by defining God as 'a being than which nothing greater can be conceived'. However, if it is the greatest, then it must be something more than merely existing in people's thoughts. We can think of something greater than a mere idea. If God is the greatest, He must really exist separately from people's thoughts. He must exist actually, in reality.

As a formal deductive argument it is:

- God is the greatest possible being (nothing greater can be conceived).
- If God exists in the mind alone (only as an idea), then a greater being could be imagined to exist both in the mind and in reality.
- This being would then be greater than God.
- Thus God cannot exist only as an idea in the mind.

Therefore, God exists both in the mind (as an idea) and in reality.

In summary, it is self-contradictory to be able to conceive of something than which nothing greater can be thought and yet to deny that that something exists.

Anselm (1033–1109)

Anselm was Italian by birth. A Benedictine monk, he later became Archbishop of Canterbury and a canonised saint of the Roman Catholic Church. He wrote many philosophical and theological works. The ontological argument appears in The Proslogion. Near the beginning is the famous statement that sums up Anselm's approach: 'I believe in order to understand.' However, there is much debate about whether Anselm was aiming his argument at believers or non-believers.

Anselm recounts how he came to the argument. He prayed for a single, short argument by which to prove almost everything about God. 'Suddenly one night during matins, the grace of God illuminated his heart. The whole matter became clear to his mind, and a great joy and exultation filled his inmost being.' What he had received was the ontological proof.

PROFILE

ii) Second form

Anselm developed his argument to demonstrate that it was impossible to conceive of God as not existing. This is the idea that God is eternal and has always been, so He is not limited by, or in, time. Put another way, Anselm argued that God had necessary existence: He could not not be. The reason is that this state is greater than a being who comes and goes out of existence. As a deductive argument it is:

- God is the greatest possible being (nothing greater can be conceived).
- It is greater to be a **necessary being** (cannot not be) than a **contingent** being (can cease to exist).

Key words

Necessary being: a being whose non-existence would be a self-contradiction. This is its sense in the ontological argument. It can also be used in the causal sense, of a being who is required as an explanation.

Contingent: that which need not be, that which could have been different; something that has dependency.

Key words

Analytic: a statement where the predicate is contained in the subject.

Synthetic: a statement where the predicate is not contained in the subject.

- If God exists only as a contingent being so can therefore be imagined not to exist, then a greater being could be imagined that cannot be conceived not to exist.
- This being would then be greater than God.
- God is therefore a necessary being.

Therefore God must exist in reality.

In summary, God must be a necessary being, meaning, He cannot not exist. Necessary here means logical necessity. It would be a logical contradiction to claim that God does not exist, since any being who has the property of necessary existence could not fail to exist.

Key thought

ANALYTIC EXISTENTIAL PROPOSITIONS

The ontological argument claims to reveal that God is a necessary being – that is, inherent in the concept of 'God' is necessary existence. When you come to analyse and examine the concept of God, it becomes clear that existence is part of the concept. Such propositions are called **analytic** and have the property that the predicate is contained in the subject. The predicate is that which is said about the subject. An example of an analytic sentence is 'All bachelors are single.' Thus 'all bachelors' is the subject and 'being single' is the predicate.

As you can see, an analytic statement does not contain any new information but clarifies the term. The surprise that the ontological argument claims to reveal is that existence is part of the concept of God. We refer to propositions that are analytic and about existence as *analytic existential propositions*. Hence 'God exists' is claimed to be an example of such a proposition.

Analytic statements can be true or false. The proposition 'All bachelors are married' is analytic but false. It is analytic because the married state is part of the concept of 'bachelor'. The fact that it is analytic does not tell you whether it is true or false, but merely how to decide whether it is true or false. The way to decide is by considering the meaning of the words.

In passing it should be noted that a sentence such as 'The cat sat on the mat' is clearly not an analytic statement, since there is nothing in the analysis of the concept of 'cat' that contains the idea of 'sitting on the mat'! Statements like these that add new information are called **synthetic**. Their truth value (that is, whether they are true or false) is determined by empirical evidence.

3 Supporters of the ontological argument

a) Descartes (1596–1650)

Key quote

God is 'a supremely perfect being, having all perfections'.

DESCARTES

Descartes is regarded as the founder of modern philosophy. In *Meditations* he proposed his philosophical arguments for a unified and certain body of human knowledge. He broke free from the dogmas of Aristotle and supported instead the new age of science.

Descartes favoured independent enquiry from first principles and asserted only that which could be known to be certain. A crucial part of his argument involved the existence of God as a guarantor for the certainty that the external world exists. The argument he uses is a form of the ontological argument:

- God, a supremely perfect being, has all perfections.
- Existence is a perfection.

Therefore God, a supremely perfect being, exists.

In *Meditation 5*, Descartes argued that there were some qualities that an object necessarily had or else it would not be that object. He considered a triangle that must have three angles adding up to 180 degrees. Equally, the notion of a hill demands the idea of a valley. In the same way, existence cannot be separated from the concept of God.

Descartes (1596–1650)

Descartes is regarded as the founder of modern philosophy. He wrote *Meditations* and in it proposed his philosophical arguments for a unified and certain body of human knowledge. He broke free from the dogmas of Aristotle and supported instead the new age of science. Descartes favoured independent enquiry from first principles and asserted only that which could be known to be certain. Key to his argument was the ontological argument to prove the existence of God, since if there was a God it would guarantee that we would not be deceived.

Key people

Norman Malcolm (1911–90) used arguments from the nature of logical necessity to reply to critics of the ontological argument.

Alvin Plantinga (b 1932) appealed to modal logic and 'possible worlds' in his ontological argument.

Key words

Possible world: anything that can be conceived of, or is logically consistent.

Modal: the mode in which something occurs, for example, either necessary or possible.

b) Recent reformulations

In the twentieth century, the ontological argument enjoyed a revival. Both Norman Malcolm in *Philosophical Review* 69 (1960) and Charles Hartshorne in *The Logic of Perfection* (1962) have centred their arguments on the idea of necessary existence. They describe it as existence which cannot be brought about or threatened by anything. Thus God's existence is either impossible or necessary. It cannot be impossible since the concept is not self-contradictory. Therefore God necessarily exists.

Alvin Plantinga in *The Nature of Necessity* (1974) has reformulated the argument using the concept of **possible worlds**. The idea of possible worlds is a popular method used by philosophers to determine the modality (necessity, impossibility or possibility) of statements. Hence this formulation of the ontological argument has become known as the **modal** form. To test for logical impossibility, these philosophers ask us to think of a possible world in which the statement is true. If you can, then the statement is not logically impossible. For a statement to be logically necessary it would have to be true in all possible worlds. So the argument goes as follows:

- There is a possible world, in which there exists a being with maximal greatness (existing in every possible world) and excellence (having the properties of omniscience, omnipotence, etc.).
- In any possible world this being has maximal excellence (omniscience, omnipotence, etc.).
- Our world is a possible world (since our world exists).

Therefore in our world there is this being!

Figure 5 Various forms of the ontological argument

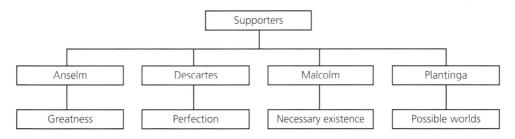

4 Criticisms of the ontological argument

The ontological argument faces a number of different criticisms.

Key question

Do we know what the word 'God' means?

a) The definition of God

This criticism argues that we do not know what the word 'God' means, or at any rate the meaning is not clear. That is why Aquinas never supported the ontological argument. He felt that such arguments for God had to be causal, based on effects that you could see and from which you could deduce that a God was required to cause them. However, most argue that the definition that Anselm used is not nonsense. It does convey meaning.

Another similar criticism argues that the definition of God is wrong. Anselm's definition is not what people see God as. However, whatever one believes about God, it seems reasonable to say that there is nothing that can be thought to be greater than God.

Perhaps a stronger criticism concerns the idea of the 'greatest or most perfect being'. Do we really have a concept of this? Indeed, is it a meaningful concept or is it like the concept of 'greatest number'? Does the property of 'most loving' have a maximum?

Key people

Aquinas (1225–74)
wrote a summary of arguments for God (*The Five Ways*) which all have as their starting point some observation or experience of the universe.

b) Logical tricks

The ontological argument attempts to pass from the thought of the existence of a thing to the actual existence of that thing. Many argue that you cannot move from a concept to reality itself, but merely to a concept of reality (see (e)).

The argument also begs the question since it makes the existence of God 'true by definition'. In addition, Malcolm's argument commits the **fallacy** of equivocation. This fallacy occurs when a word is used in two different senses. The word misused by Malcolm is 'impossible'. He is accused of using it both in the sense of a matter of fact (unable to come about) and also in the sense of being logically contradictory. Malcolm concludes in his argument that God is necessary in the former sense (factual) whereas He is 'necessary' in the latter sense (logical). As a result, what the argument does show is that *if* God exists, then God exists necessarily, but not *that* God exists.

Plantinga's argument merely shows that God is possible, not that He is actual. Others point out that if you can have a being with maximal greatness and excellence, then what results from arguing for a possible world where no being exemplifies maximal greatness?

Perhaps an even more radical criticism is to disagree with the proposition that to deny that God exists involves a self-contradiction, on the basis that logic is purely an arbitrary linguistic convention that tells us nothing about reality.

c) Existence is not a great-making quality

One of the major opponents of the ontological argument was Immanuel Kant. He made the point that existence is not a real **predicate** – it does not tell us what an object is like (that is, some quality or characteristic). Kant felt that 'exist' was a word that merely stated that a concept had an actuality. It did not actually add anything to the concept. The real contains no more than the merely possible, so a concept is not made greater by adding reality.

Kant expressed it like this, in his book *The Critique of Pure Reason* (1781):

> If we take the subject (God) with all its predicates (e.g. all knowledge), and say 'God is' or 'There is a God', we attach no new predicate to the concept of God … merely posit it as being an object that stands in relation to my concept. The content of both must be one and the same … The real contains no more than the merely possible. A hundred real thalers do not contain the least coin more than a hundred possible thalers. [A thaler was an old German silver coin.]

Brian Davies in *Thinking about God* (1985) has expressed the same point using a different example:

For someone who claims to compare two things, one of which exists and the other of which does not, is just not doing what he says he is doing. If we contrast (or compare) A with B, then both A and B must exist. A non-existent book is not different from a real book. Nor is it similar. It is just not there to be either similar or different to anything. Hence as Kant said 'Being' is the positing of a thing.

Key question

Does existence add anything to a concept?

We do not add anything to the concept when we declare that it 'is'. Otherwise it would not be exactly the same thing that exists but something more than we had thought in the concept; and we could not, therefore, say that the exact object of my concept exists.

Thus many regard 'exists' more as a number. To say that something exists is to deny the number zero. Bertrand Russell made a similar point. He used the example of 'cows exist' but 'unicorns do not exist'. He said that we are not talking about cows and saying that they have the attribute of existence or that unicorns lack this attribute. Rather we are talking of the concepts of a cow and a unicorn and saying that one of them has an instance and one of them does not.

Key people

Bertrand Russell (1872–1970) was a British philosopher who pioneered 'linguistic philosophy' which centred on the task of establishing the meaning of statements.

It was because Malcolm felt that existence was not a great-making quality that he was led to develop his form of the ontological argument based more closely on Anselm's second form. Malcolm argued that necessary being is a property, namely the property of an inability to be generated or made corrupt.

However, supporters of the ontological argument have responded to such criticisms, arguing that existence can be a real predicate. Stephen Davis (*God, Reason and Theistic Proofs*, 1997) notes that:

Key quote

'"Being" is the positing of a thing.'
KANT

Of the real hundred thalers, my concept of them includes the property of having-purchasing-power-in-the-real-world. My concept of a hundred thalers does not have that property.

d) You cannot have an analytic existential proposition

We defined an analytic proposition on page 23. An analytic existential proposition is an analytic statement about existence. Many philosophers argue that propositions about existence are not analytic but synthetic and contingent. If this is correct, then the ontological argument has been guilty of some logical tricks since its conclusion appears to be an existential analytic statement, namely 'God exists'.

Key question

Is it possible to have an analytic existential proposition?

In reply, supporters of the ontological argument have argued that it is possible to have analytic existential propositions. They cite such examples as 'A number greater than a million exists' and 'Science fiction characters do not exist' as analytic existential propositions. The debate continues…!

Key question

Is it possible to move from a definition to proving an existence?

Key people

Gaunilo (or Gaunilon)
was an eleventh-century Benedictine monk and contemporary of Anselm. He is primarily known for his criticism of Anselm's ontological argument and used the illustration of a 'lost island'.

Key quote

'... there is no contradiction in rejecting the triangle together with its three angles.'

KANT

e) You cannot define things into existence

Even if one were to accept that existence was a great-making property, some philosophers still feel that the argument fails. This is because the thrust of the ontological argument seems to be that by defining God you can be assured of His existence. To most, such an idea seems absurd. It implies you can define anything into existence. There seems to be some intellectual sleight of hand involved in moving from a definition to proving an existence.

Many feel that 'filling out a concept' and 'showing that there really is something to which the concept refers' are two quite different processes and that the first does *not* lead to the second. Remember that the ontological argument alleges that we cannot explain the concept of God properly without coming to the conclusion that He exists.

This apparent flaw in the argument was noted by a monk called Gaunilo, at the time of Anselm. He used the illustration of a 'lost island' that was the most excellent of all islands. He argued that though he could easily form the concept in his mind, it would be absurd to conclude therefore that such an island existed in reality. The thrust of the argument is that if the existence of God can be proved in this way, then the existence of anything (such as a lost island) can also be proved.

In reply, Anselm argued that islands are contingent and therefore do not have necessary existence as an aspect of their properties. However, God does. Indeed, God is unique in this aspect. Existence is not part of the greatness of an island, whereas necessary existence is part of the concept of God. Hence to say that 'God does not exist' is the same thing as saying 'An existing God does not exist'. Such a statement is nonsense. The reason why the above is nonsense is that contradiction results from negating the predicate of a true analytic statement.

Kant proposed that no such contradiction arose if you rejected both subject and predicate, 'for nothing is left that you can contradict'. Kant expressed it in these words (*The Critique of Pure Reason*, trans N Kemp Smith, 1965):

> *It would be self-contradictory to posit a triangle and yet reject its three angles, but there is no contradiction in rejecting the triangle together with its three angles.*

Thus if we were to look again at Gaunilo's criticism of Anselm, then he appears to be saying that it is not a contradiction to claim that there is not a being who in reality exists that has the property of necessary existence.

Definitions only tell us what God would be like *if* He existed. They cannot establish whether He does in fact exist. One can move from a concept of imagination to a concept of reality but not from a concept of imagination to reality. Hence there is no contradiction in denying the reality of a conceptual being who has necessary existence.

When we say that existence is part of God's definition, we are merely saying that no non-existing being can be God. To put it another way, if God exists He will have necessary existence, but it is not a contradiction to say that such a concept does not have an actuality.

Hume said in *Dialogues concerning Natural Religion* that:

> *However much our concept of an object may contain, we must go outside of it to determine whether or not it exists. We cannot define something into existence – even if it has all the perfections we can imagine.*

As you may have guessed, this view has not gone unchallenged. Some people have pointed out that explaining a concept can make non-existence apparent. Take, for example, 'round squares'. These cannot exist. A concept leads to a non-existence. So perhaps the two processes of concept and actuality are related and therefore *perhaps* it is possible that by filling out a concept you can move to actuality. All is very teasing, and hence the debate continues.

f) Conclusions

It seems that the ontological argument is insufficient to convert the atheist, since it appears to fail as a proof. However, perhaps that was not its original intention. It is likely that Anselm was writing for those who already had a belief in God, and thus to show that their faith was rational. Indeed, he says in the preface to his *Proslogion*:

> *I have written the following treatise in the person of one who … seeks to understand what he believes …*

At best one can say that if God exists, He will have necessary existence, *but* perhaps that does not prove that He does exist. A new development in the ontological debate involves seeing God *not* as an object but rather as a grammatical observation. This new approach will be discussed in chapter 9. One thing does seem certain – the last word has yet to be said about the ontological argument.

Key quote

'We cannot define something into existence – even if it has all the perfections we can imagine.'
HUME

Key question

Are the two processes of concept and actuality related?

Key question

What was Anselm's intention in presenting the ontological argument?

Figure 6 Strengths and weaknesses of the ontological argument

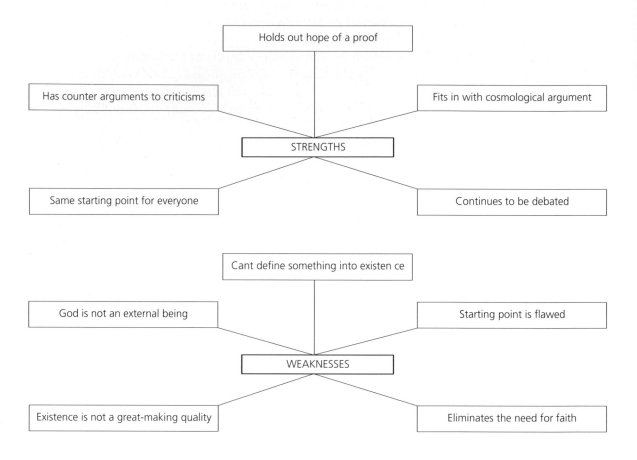

Study guide

By the end of this chapter you should know and understand the forms of the ontological argument by Anselm and Descartes as well as at least one of the modern forms of the argument. You should know and understand the main weaknesses of the arguments and be able to explain clearly how they weaken the argument. Some responses to those criticisms should also be known.

Revision checklist

Can you name **five** scholars connected with the ontological arguments, and can you state whether each supports or opposes the argument?

Can you explain how each of the following words/phrases is connected to the ontological argument?

- Analytic
- Existence
- Great-making quality
- Predicate.

Do you know the difference between the following?

- Deductive–inductive
- A priori–a posteriori
- Analytic–synthetic
- Anselm's argument–Descartes' argument.

Can you give **two** arguments on each side on the following questions?

- Is the ontological argument proof of God's existence?
- Does the ontological argument have more strengths than weaknesses?

Examples of exam questions

1 a) Outline Descartes' ontological argument for the existence of God.

b) Its strengths are greater than its weaknesses. Discuss.

In part a), the lower level AO1 answer would just state the basic definition and that existence is a perfection, concluding that God must therefore exist. Higher level answers would express the argument in argument form and explain it. Reference might also be made to Descartes' illustrations of the three angles adding up to 180 degrees and the notion of a valley, linking them to the argument that existence cannot be separated from the concept of God.

The b) part is AO2 skill. Lower level answers would tend to list the strengths and the weaknesses. Higher level answers would involve some comparisons and weighing one against the other.

2 Discuss how far Anselm's ontological argument proves the existence of God.

This involves both an AO1 element of showing knowledge and understanding of Anselm's ontological argument, and an AO2 element of assessing whether such an argument is a proof. Lower level answers will tend just to give a general outline of the ontological argument. Higher levels will show understanding by explaining the argument and possibly expressing it in argument form. Higher level answers on the AO2 skill will discuss what constitutes philosophical proof and relate it to the ontological deductive argument.

Further questions to consider

1 Outline the ontological argument for the existence of God and consider the view that, while it may strengthen a believer's faith, it has no value for the non-believer.

2 How successfully do the ontological argument and the argument from experience counter the claim that God exists only in the mind?

4

THE EXISTENCE OF GOD – 2
THE COSMOLOGICAL ARGUMENT

Chapter checklist

This chapter covers the classical three forms of the cosmological argument for the existence of God by Aquinas. Two other forms – the principle of sufficient reason and the beginnings argument – are also discussed. In addition, there is a summary of Copleston's famous radio debate with Bertrand Russell. The arguments are evaluated in respect of their strengths and weaknesses and the extent to which they can be considered a proof for God.

1 The cosmological argument

a) Historical background

The **cosmological** argument attempts to infer the existence of God from the existence of the cosmos or from phenomena within it. The claim is that the universe cannot account for its own existence and so this argument seeks causes that have their solution in the existence of a God. It is an argument that has a long history. In *Timaeus*, Plato says that every created thing must be created by some cause. The argument is also found in Aristotle's works. Aquinas presented the popular form in the first three of his Five Ways. Further support was given by Descartes and Leibniz. In his book *Theodicy* (1710), Leibniz said that the great principle of the cosmological argument is that 'nothing takes place without sufficient reason'. Its modern proponents who argue that it has some degree of probability are Craig and Swinburne. Its main opponents have been Hume and Kant.

b) Aquinas' arguments

St Thomas Aquinas (1225–74) wrote a number of arguments for the existence of God. They have become known as the Five Ways. The first three 'ways' are different variations of the cosmological argument:

- The Unmoved Mover.
- The Uncaused Causer.
- Possibility and Necessity.

i) The First Way – The Unmoved Mover (The Unchanged Changer/The Prime Mover)

Key question

What type of 'movement' did Aquinas mean in the phrase 'The Unmoved Mover'?

There are various types of motion (change): change of place, change of size and change of state. It is the last one that Aquinas had particularly in mind. Here movement has the sense of moving from potentiality to actuality. For instance, wood is potentially hot, and for a piece of wood to become hot it has to be changed by fire. What is potentially x is not actually x, yet the actually x can only be produced by something that is actually x. Whatever is moved (changed) must be moved (changed) by another, which itself was moved (changed). If we trace back we must arrive at a first mover, moved by no other. This is what we understand to be God. Expressed formally:

- Everything that is in motion (change) is moved (changed) by something else.
- Infinite regress is impossible.

Therefore there must be a first mover (changer).

Aquinas was not arguing that the universe necessarily had a beginning. He thought it did, but said that you could not reason that out as it was revealed doctrine. Rather his emphasis was on dependency. This dependency argument is one that has reappeared in the twentieth century and is taken up by Swinburne. Christian theology has always taught that God sustains the universe. In other words, if God ceased to exist then the universe would also cease. Therefore there must be an initiator of the change whose continued existence is depended upon. In the same way, a play depends on the continued existence of actors. This type of causal relationship is what Aquinas had in mind.

Key question

Did Aquinas argue that the universe had to have a beginning?

Key people

Richard Swinburne (b 1934) is an Oxford professor of philosophy who has devoted himself to promoting arguments for theism.

ii) The Second Way – The Uncaused Causer (The First Cause Argument)

This follows a similar line of argument but replaces motion (change) with cause:

- Every effect has a cause.
- Infinite regress is impossible.

Therefore there must be a first cause.

In other words, everything that happens has a cause. The cause itself has a cause. Something cannot cause itself for this would mean it preceded itself and this is impossible. Hence the need for an uncaused causer, namely God.

One of the differences between these two 'ways' is that in the first, attention is centred on the fact that things are acted upon, whereas in the second, the attention is on things as agents (doing the acting upon). The first cause sees God as a factual necessity, as the causal explanation to the universe. This means that God is seen as a being who is not dependent on any other for His existence. He is a contingent being that is causeless, and it would not be a logical contradiction if such a being did not actually exist. This is in contrast to the ontological argument that sees God as a logically necessary being. Remember that in the case of a logically necessary being, it would be a logical contradiction to claim that it did not exist.

Thomas Aquinas (1225–74)

St Thomas Aquinas has been a very influential philosopher and theologian who is especially highly regarded by Roman Catholics. He lived at a time when a renewed interest in Aristotle coincided with a view that philosophy could be useful to Christian theology, to demonstrate the reasonableness of faith and also to help explore articles of faith. Hence Aquinas attempted to apply the philosophy of Aristotle to Christianity. The philosophy of Aquinas is often referred to by the name 'Thomism'. He wrote prolifically and in *Summa Theologica*, a book containing over 4000 pages, Aquinas devoted only two pages to his arguments for the existence of God. However, their compact form has made them popular, and they have become known as the Five Ways:

- The Unmoved Mover.
- The Uncaused Causer.
- Possibility and Necessity.
- Goodness, Truth and Nobility.
- Teleological.

These five arguments are all a posteriori and have as their starting point some observation or experience of the universe. The first three 'ways' are different variations of the cosmological argument.

iii) The Third Way – Possibility and Necessity (Contingency)

Key word

A contingent being: a being, such that if it exists, it cannot exist.

For Aquinas, anything that had a property was referred to as a 'being'. The world consists of **contingent** items, that is, beings that are generated and perish (see page 23). If all beings were contingent, then at one time nothing would have existed. This is because there would have been a time prior to the coming into existence of contingent beings. But if that is the case, then nothing would be able to come into existence as everything contingent has a prior cause.

Thus all beings cannot be contingent. There must exist **a necessary being**, which Aquinas refers to as God. Again, expressed formally:

- Some contingent beings exist.
- If any contingent beings exist then a necessary being must exist.

Therefore a necessary being exists, namely God.

2 Criticisms of Aquinas' arguments

- Some scholars have argued that Aquinas' arguments rest on assumptions that are no longer widely held. Ancient and medieval science thought in terms of a hierarchy of causes, which is different to modern-day thinking. It is an assumption that actual x can only be brought about by what is actual x. For example, two cold objects rubbed together will cause heat.
- Why cannot there be an endless series of causes? In reply Mackie (*The Miracle of Theism*, 1982, p. 90) cites the analogy of a railway train consisting of an infinite number of carriages. Each carriage may move the next carriage but ultimately it only makes sense if there is an engine. The problem then becomes one of demonstrating that Aquinas' three ways have such a relation of dependence.
- Why cannot there be some contingent items that have lasted through all past time and will show their contingency by perishing at some time in the future?
- If nothing can cause itself, how can God be seen as an uncaused causer? In reply it is stated that the cause of the universe must lie in something outside it. Thus Aquinas did not see God as just another thing like everything else in the universe, but bigger. Rather, God is of a totally different order and not subject to the same conditions as the universe.
- Why a single termination? Why must the regress lead to one first cause? Independent happenings might lead back to causes which are independent of each other. Therefore there would not be a single first cause but a plurality of first causes.
- Why cannot the different forms of the three ways lead to a different 'God' for each? Why should they lead to God as understood in the Christian concept? Indeed, why should God not be the originator and now no longer exist? After all, a mother causes a child but then dies.
- The argument begins with 'this world' and concludes with concepts of which we have no experience, for example, uncaused, infinity.
- The universe is not contingent, that is, matter or energy in the universe is eternal. Particular objects come and go, but the matter

of which they are composed is forever and exists necessarily. It could not have failed to exist. There is not a reason – it is just brute fact. Thus the great ultimates of the universe are about matter, not about a metaphysical being called God.

● In reply it is argued that since everything in the universe is contingent, everything could cease to exist simultaneously, and then the universe itself would cease. But if it can cease to exist, then it must be contingent. Recent thinking in physics has also questioned the eternal nature of matter.

Figure 7 Aquinas' three ways of the cosmological argument

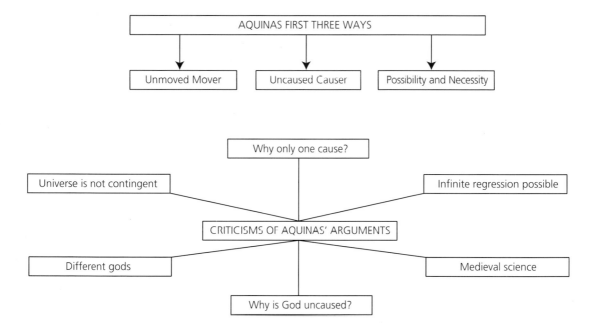

3 Other forms of the cosmological argument

Key people

Leibniz (1646–1716)
Most scholars regard Leibniz's philosophy as wide ranging and, in parts, very complex. One idea that he made popular was that of the principle of sufficient reason. This states that for everything that is the case, there must be a reason why it is the case.

a) The principle of sufficient reason

Leibniz (1646–1716) avoided the problem of infinite regression by reinterpreting the endless series, not of events, but of explanations. Even if the universe had always existed, there is nothing within the universe to show *why* it exists. According to Leibniz, everything has a sufficient reason.

The principle of sufficient reason states that, in the case of any positive truth, there is some sufficient reason for it: in other words, there is some sort of explanation, known or unknown, for everything. The world does not seem to contain within itself the reason for its own existence. Therefore God exists.

Key people

Frederick Copleston (1907–94)
was a Jesuit priest and philosopher who wrote an influential book about Aquinas' Five Ways as well as a nine-volume *History of Philosophy*.

Bertrand Russell (1872–1970)
was a British philosopher who pioneered 'linguistic philosophy' which centred on the task of establishing the meaning of statements.

b) Copleston's radio debate

In 1948 a radio debate was broadcast in which Frederick Copleston and Bertrand Russell discussed the cosmological argument. The form of the argument that Copleston defended was one based on contingency and the principle of sufficient reason. The key steps in his argument were:

- There are at least some beings in the world which do not contain in themselves the reason for their existence.
- The totality of the world comprises of such objects. There is no world distinct from these objects.
- The explanation for the world must therefore be found external to it.
- The reason must ultimately be an existent being which contains within itself the reason for its own existence.
- The reason is that it cannot not exist. It is a necessary being – God.

In other words, only God, a necessary being, can be the complete explanation for the existence of the universe that contains contingent items. It is the explanation that requires no further explanation.

Some 200 years earlier, David Hume had argued that it was illegitimate to move from saying that every event in the universe has a cause to the claim that the universe has a cause. Bertrand Russell made a similar point by remarking that this was like moving from saying that every human being has a mother to the claim that the human race as a whole has a mother. One cannot move from individual causes to the claim that the totality has a cause.

In his book *Why I am not a Christian* (1957, p. 140) Russell says, 'The universe is just there, and that's all there is to say.' However, we ask 'why' of things within the universe, therefore it seems consistent to ask why the universe itself is there. The theist assumes that the universe is intelligible and ultimately depends on an eternal self-existent reality. Copleston likened Russell's approach of denying the problem to saying 'If one refuses to even sit down at the chess board and make a move, one cannot, of course, be checkmated.'

Key quotes

'The universe is just there, and that's all there is to say.'
BERTRAND RUSSELL

'If one refuses to even sit down at the chess board and make a move, one cannot, of course, be checkmated.'
FREDERICK COPLESTON

c) The beginning argument

People often say that 'things cannot have got going by themselves'. This argument can be called 'the beginning argument', and is sometimes referred to as the Kalam cosmological argument, popular in Islam. Its origins date back to about 850CE to a group which belonged to the Islamic Kalam tradition of philosophy. However, the argument was used by John Locke (1632–1704) and has had a revival in the late twentieth century, mainly through the writings of William Craig. This argument claims that everything that begins to

Key people

William Craig (b 1949)
is a strong defender of Christian theism. He is often credited with reviving the Kalam cosmological argument.

Key question

Did the universe have a beginning or has it always existed?

Key question

Can something come into existence without a cause?

Key word

Big Bang theory: the theory of an expanding universe that began as an infinitely dense and hot medium at some finite time in the past. The initial instant is called the Big Bang.

Key quote

'An expanding universe does not preclude a creator, but it does place limits on when he might have carried out his job!'

STEPHEN HAWKING

Key word

Oscillating universe theory: the theory that there has been an infinite series of expanding and contracting universes.

exist has a cause of its existence, and since the universe began to exist, the universe has a cause of its existence. Transcending the entire universe there exists a cause which brought the universe into being. This cause is God.

Attempts have been made to destroy the argument by claiming that it is possible to imagine something coming into existence without a cause. However, you can only know whether something began to exist if it has a cause. If not, how do you know it did not exist elsewhere?

Support for something without a cause has recently come from subatomic physics. Here it appears that electrons can pass out of existence at one point and then come back into existence elsewhere without any cause. In reply, some argue that this phenomenon results from the limits of our investigative equipment, that is, our present scientific knowledge stops us finding the cause, but there is one.

The main debate therefore tends to revolve around the assumption that the universe had a beginning. Certainly modern cosmology suggests the **Big Bang theory** which implies a finite past history of the universe, even if it does not imply finite time. Support for such a theory includes the evidence that the universe is expanding, which suggests that it had a starting point.

Philosophically speaking, if the universe had no beginning, then an actual infinite number of past moments of the universe's history have elapsed, and they are being added to as time goes on. But one cannot add to an infinite number of things. For instance, if there is an infinite number of dogs, then one cannot add to that number of dogs by introducing another dog. Likewise, if there has elapsed an infinite number of past moments of the universe, then this number cannot be added to either. Yet the universe continues to exist. Moments continue to be added. This implies that the universe had a beginning. Further, if the universe had no beginning, then an infinity of years will have been traversed, which is impossible.

Needless to say, the above arguments have been challenged. For example, it is argued that:

- Modern cosmology allows for an infinite past history of the universe since it is consistent with the evidence to have an infinite series of expanding and contracting universes. This is known as the **oscillating universe theory**.

- Many argue that it is to misunderstand the word 'infinity' to treat it as though it were a number. Rather it is a concept. Hence it is meaningless to speak of 'adding more moments of time' or 'traversing infinite years'.
- If there were no starting point, then from any specific point in past time there is only a finite stretch that needs to be traversed to reach the present.

Key question

Could God cease to be?

Given that the universe had a beginning, some philosophers question whether God must be the cause. Even if God did start it, God could then cease to be. This is very far from the traditional view that God not only began the world but sustains it, and that without God things would cease to be.

4 Conclusions

The cosmological argument does not force the atheist to become a theist, since the atheist can still claim that the universe has no ultimate explanation but is just a brute fact. Hence it can only point to the *possibility* of God. It does bring into sharp contrast the two ways of looking at the universe – namely that it is inexplicable or that it is intelligible. If there is an explanation, it is possible that it could be contained in 'God'.

Study guide

By the end of this chapter you should know and understand the three forms of the cosmological argument by Aquinas as well as the forms based on the principle of sufficient reason and beginnings. You should know and understand the main weaknesses of the arguments and be able to explain clearly how they weaken the argument. Some responses to those criticisms should also be known.

Revision checklist

Can you name **five** scholars connected with the cosmological arguments, and can you state whether each supports or opposes the argument?

Can you explain how each of the following words/phrases is connected to the cosmological argument?

- Infinite regression
- Brute fact
- Big Bang theory
- Principle of sufficient reason.

Do you know the difference between the following?

- Unmoved mover–uncaused causer
- Potential–actual
- Necessary–contingent.

Can you give **two** arguments on each side on the following issues?

- Is the cosmological argument proof of God's existence?
- Does the cosmological argument have more strengths than weaknesses?

Example of exam question

Outline the cosmological argument for the existence of God and assess its claim to prove that God exists.

The AO1 element requires showing knowledge and understanding of the argument. No particular argument is specified by name so it is up to the candidate to choose which one (or more) they feel most confident to write about. Remember this is only part of the question so the time allocated needs to be kept in mind. Lower level answers will be brief statements of the argument and lack any real explanation. Higher level answers might have the argument expressed and discussed in its correct argument form in terms of premises and conclusion. Higher level answers will also explain the reasoning of the argument.

The AO2 needs some discussion about proof. Higher level answers will discuss in terms of inductive and deductive arguments, linking it to the cosmological argument form. There will be a weighing up of the strength of the argument and some conclusion drawn in terms of a lesser or greater probability of God's existence. Higher level answers will explain the difference between probability and proof.

Further questions to consider

1 Discuss the extent to which the cosmological argument for the existence of God offers a coherent explanation of the universe.

2 Outline the cosmological argument for the existence of God. Examine criticisms that have been made of its form, content and conclusions.

5 THE EXISTENCE OF GOD – 3 THE TELEOLOGICAL ARGUMENT

Chapter checklist

This chapter covers the classical forms of the teleological argument for the existence of God by Aquinas and Paley. A modern form by Swinburne is also discussed as is the anthropic form of the design argument. The arguments are then evaluated in respect of their strengths and weaknesses and the extent to which they can be considered a proof for God.

1 Introduction

Key words

Teleological: explanation by reference to end or purpose.

Anthropic argument: nature planning in advance for the needs of humans.

Analogy: a comparison of two or more things to show how they are similar.

The cosmological argument attempted to infer the existence of God from the existence of the cosmos. What it really did was to look at a feature of the universe, namely that the universe cannot account for its own existence. The teleological argument is similar in approach. Probably the most popular and most often expressed by people, it infers the existence of God from a particular aspect or character of the world, namely the presence of order, regularity and purpose. Order, regularity and purpose are seen as marks of design, and the argument concludes that God must be the source of that design. The kind of thing that is usually appealed to as evidence of order in the universe is the solar system, with the planets revolving in their predictable orbits, or the human eye.

The word **teleological** is derived from the Greek word *telos* meaning 'end' or 'purpose'. Thus nature is viewed as directed in order that something beneficial may result. More popularly it is referred to as the 'argument from design', but this wording assumes the very thing that has to be proved. A better description would be the 'argument for design'.

Design arguments are a posteriori and there are various types of argument, with different philosophers giving them different names. Swinburne identifies the argument from design *and* the argument to design (also known as the **anthropic argument**). The former is the popular form usually involving **analogy**. The latter involves arguing that nature provides for the needs of intelligent beings. This provision requires an intelligence – God.

2 The argument from design

This argument has been used down the ages. For instance, Plato suggested that mind ordered all things. Nevertheless certain philosophers are particularly associated with the argument.

a) St Thomas Aquinas (1225–74)

Aquinas (see page 35) features this argument as the fifth of his Five Ways. The heart of this argument is that non-intelligent material things produce beneficial order, and therefore require an intelligent being to bring this about, that is, God. Aquinas' views about nature included thinking that things develop toward the realisation of ends that are internal to their own natures. An archer must direct an arrow. In the same way God must direct nature. Aquinas argued that there cannot be purposefulness without a guiding intelligence.

Key question

Can there be purposefulness without a guiding intelligence?

b) David Hume (1711–76)

One of the classical statements of the argument, and one that particularly reflects eighteenth-century thinking, appears in Hume's *Dialogues concerning Natural Religion*. His book was written in the form of a dialogue between three main characters. Hence, two characters express the argument for design and then Hume, through another character (Philo), criticises the argument. This criticism is thought to be Hume's real view. However, he does give a fair presentation of the case for design:

> *Look round the world: Contemplate the whole and every part of it: You will find it to be nothing but one great machine, subdivided into an infinite number of lesser machines … All these various machines, and even their most minute parts are adjusted to one another with an accuracy, which ravishes into administration all men, who have ever contemplated them. The curious adapting of means to ends, throughout all nature, resembles exactly, though it much exceeds, the productions of human contrivance; of human design, thought, wisdom, and intelligence. Since therefore the effects resemble each other we are led to infer, by the rules of analogy, that the causes also resemble; and that the Author of nature is somewhat similar to the mind of man; though possessed of much larger faculties, proportional to the grandeur of the work, which He has executed. By this argument a posteriori, we do prove at once the existence of a Deity, and his similarity to human mind and intelligence. (p. 22)*

Key quote

'Since therefore the effects resemble each other we are led to infer, by the rules of analogy, that the causes also resemble; and that the Author of nature is somewhat similar to the mind of man …'

HUME

This appeal to analogy was the popular form of expressing the argument. It was based on the argument that similar effects imply similar causes. What counted as marks of design are those features in which natural objects resemble machines made by human beings: the fitting of parts and what can be seen as the adaptation of means to ends. Three kinds of these features particularly impressed eighteenth-century thinkers: the world as a whole, especially the solar system as described by Newton's gravitational theory; the bodies of all sorts of plants and animals, especially certain organs like the eye; and the providential arrangement of things on the Earth.

One of the man-made objects which impressed people at that time was the pocket watch, which had just been invented. In his *Dialogue 5*, Hume uses the analogy of houses and watches, because they are so clearly produced by human designers. He says the world is like a house or a watch or a collection of houses or watches, therefore it is probably produced by something like a human designer. As has been noted, the purpose of his writing was in fact to criticise the argument, and to these criticisms we shall return later.

c) William Paley (1743–1805)

Hume's *Dialogues* was actually published in 1779, after Hume had died. William Paley wrote his book *Natural Theology* in 1802 and, though he never refers to Hume, it is thought that he included an attempt at answering the criticisms that Hume had made of the design argument. He uses the analogy of the watch (for which he is particularly remembered, though, as we have seen, it is by no means original). Suppose you are crossing a heath and come across a watch. Paley argued that even if you had never seen a watch before, you would know that this instrument did not happen by chance, but must be the result of the work of an intelligent mind. All the parts fit together and achieve the purpose of telling the time. The watch must have had an intelligent and skilled maker who designed it to do what it does. The watch demands a watchmaker, and no entirely naturalistic explanation would be acceptable. Likewise, the way the universe fits together for a purpose demands an intelligent designer. The designer would have to be God.

Paley also supported his argument by giving further examples of complex purposeful design found in nature. For instance, he referred to the eye as being designed for the particular purpose of seeing. Paley regards both the watch and the universe as teleological systems that require an intelligent mind to bring them into being.

William Paley (1743–1805)

Paley became Archdeacon of Carlisle. He argued that human beings had the capacity to reason from the natural world about God's existence. Equally he believed in the necessity of revelation for grasping certain Christian doctrines. He is particularly famous for his watch analogy. It is interesting that in Darwin's autobiography, he refers to Paley: 'In order to pass the B.A. examination, it was, also, necessary to get up Paley's *Evidences of Christianity*, and his *Moral Philosophy* … The logic of this book and as I may add of his *Natural Theology* gave me as much delight as did Euclid …'

Besides purpose, Paley also argued that the regularity observed in the universe required the idea of an intelligent mind as explanation. He used as evidence scientific findings from his own time, from astronomy and from Newton's laws. An instance of this was the way the planets obeyed laws in their movements. The whole universe and all its parts seemed ordered and acted in a regular and predictable way according to fundamental laws. The agent responsible for such order must be God.

d) Richard Swinburne (b 1934)

Swinburne acknowledges that the argument from spatial order, used by Paley and Hume, is not very persuasive. By spatial order, Swinburne means the complex structures of things such as plants and animals. In *The Existence of God* (1979), he refers to 'the subtle and coherent arrangement of their millions of parts' (p. 134) and calls this spatial order 'the regularities of co-presence'. It is not persuasive, because such ordered complexities can be explained by modern science (theory of natural selection) and so does not require the introduction of a God.

However, Swinburne focuses on temporal order (what he calls regularities of succession). By temporal order he means the laws of nature throughout the universe. The universe is orderly, yet it could have been chaotic. Nature seems to conform to a formula. If there is an explanation to account for this, then it cannot be a scientific one because we explain the operation of scientific laws in terms of more general scientific laws. Swinburne concludes:

> So either the orderliness of nature is where all explanation stops, or we must postulate an agent of great power and knowledge … the simplest such agent is … God. (pp. 140–41)

Intelligent design

This is a relatively recent addition to the debate and argues that an intelligence is necessary to explain the complex, information-rich structures of biology, and that this intelligence is empirically detectable. The evidence includes irreducible complexities.

Key people

Richard Swinburne (b 1934) is an Oxford professor of philosophy who has devoted himself to promoting arguments for theism.

Key quote

'So either the orderliness of nature is where all explanation stops, or we must postulate an agent of great power and knowledge … the simplest such agent is … God.'
SWINBURNE

Key word

Intelligent design: the view that an intelligent cause (which is not identified) accounts for certain features of the universe. Its supporters claim that it is a 'scientific' theory.

Key word

Irreducible complexity: when all parts of a system must be in place in order for the system to work. The removal of any one of the parts causes the system to stop functioning.

Key people

Michael Behe (b 1952) is a professor of biochemistry who termed the concept 'irreducible complexity'.

Key question

Is 'intelligent design' scientific?

Irreducible complexity means that all the parts of a system must be in place at once for the system to work. The different parts could not have arisen separately or by gradual change. The claim is that there are examples of such complexities in our biochemical systems. The originator of this approach is Michael Behe. Intelligent design supporters claim that their approach is a more adequate scientific explanation of the biological evidence than the theory of evolution. It does not say anything about the nature of the source of design, though it could be seen as pointing towards theism.

Philosophical ways to express the argument

This argument could be formally stated in a variety of ways. C Stephen Evans in *Thinking about Faith* (1985) suggests one that centres on the analogy aspect:

- Objects in nature are analogous to man-made machines.
- Man-made machines are the result of intelligent design.
- Analogous effects will have analogous causes.

Therefore objects in nature are the result of something analogous to intelligent design.

The argument from design really consists of two steps:

- Showing that the world exhibits 'apparent design' (the characteristics of order, regularity, effectiveness, purpose, benefit, for example).
- Inferring from this apparent design, by analogy, an intelligent cause.

3 The argument to design

Key word

Anthropic argument: nature planning in advance for the needs of humans.

Key quote

'As we look out into the Universe and identify the many accidents of physics and astronomy that have worked to our benefit, it almost seems as if the Universe must in some sense have known that we were coming.'

DYSON

This is also referred to as the **anthropic argument** or the argument from providence or the argument from beauty. It argues that nature seems to plan in advance for the needs of animals and humans. This planning cannot be accounted for by physical laws alone since there are innumerable ways that electrons could run. There must be more than physical laws to account for the improbability of life. It suggests mind or intelligence. Like the form of the argument by analogy, it lends itself more to an inductive formulation than to a deductive one.

Some modern proponents have argued that modern developments in science, rather than weakening the teleological argument, have lent support to it. Appeal is made to the intricate relationships found in biochemistry relating to the development of living organisms, and evolution, suggesting that this could not have occurred by accident, but rather required some overall direction.

Key question

Could the cosmological constants have been different?

Key word

Planck's constant: used in Quantam mechanics to describe the sizes of quanta.

Key quote

'If it can be demonstrated that any complex organ existed, which could not possibly have been formed by numerous, successive, slight modifications, my theory would absolutely break down.'

DARWIN

It looks like things have worked together to our benefit, almost as if the universe in some sense had known that we were coming. S Davis (*God, Reason and Theistic Proofs*, 1997) lists a number of examples that seem to be fine-tuned for life. Included in his examples (pp. 108–11) are:

- Cosmological constants – these are items like the gravitational constant, the speed of light, the basic properties of elementary particles, and **Planck's constant**. All these constants could have been different, yet their values all fall within a very narrow range that makes life possible.
- The rate of expansion of the Big Bang – this focuses on the speed at which bits of matter flew apart from other bits of matter soon after the Big Bang. Galaxies would have been impossible had the expansion rate and total mass of universe not been finely tuned to each other.
- Thermal properties of water – if the Earth were either five per cent closer or one per cent further from the Sun, life would not be possible. The Earth has an atmosphere, which protects it from ultra-radiation; and oceans serve as a thermostat shielding us from extreme temperatures.

Similar arguments speak in terms of 'probability', concluding that the order of the universe is, statistically speaking, 'beyond chance'. Often terms such as 'an anti-chance factor' are introduced. In 1985, the then Bishop of Birmingham, Hugh Montefiore, wrote a book called *The Probability of God*. This argued that, given the findings of science, the most reasonable explanation for the character of the universe is God.

In a similar vein, FR Tennant (*Philosophical Theology*, 1930) argues that the universe is not just beautiful in places; it is saturated with beauty from the microscopic to the macroscopic level. Likewise, Swinburne argues in terms of probabilities and God being the simplest explanation to account for the universe.

Figure 8 The teleological argument

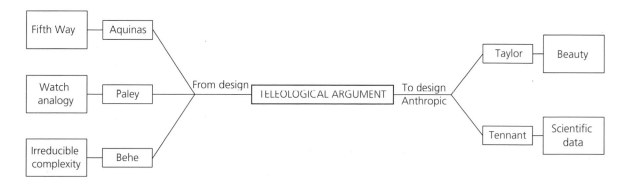

4 Hume's criticisms

a) An initial difficulty

Before dealing in detail with Hume's criticisms, it is worth noting a general point of confusion about the analogy approach. It is by no means clear in the analogy whether the machine, etc. is being compared to:

(i)   the whole of the universe or
(ii) parts of the universe.

If it is (i) then how can you say that the whole of the universe is working to an end or purpose? It certainly is not obvious. Many argue that to conclude such a thing requires knowledge obtainable only from being outside the universe (although it could be obtained by revelation).

Alternatively, in (ii) it may be possible to show that parts of the universe work to an end or purpose, *but* it is a **fallacy** of logic to then argue from that, that the whole works to a particular end or purpose.

b) Hume's criticisms

Hume worked on his critique of the argument of design for some 25 years, culminating in his now famous book *Dialogues concerning Natural Religion*. Some of his friends urged him to abandon it or even destroy it, regarding it as too dangerous and irreligious. However, he made plans for it to be published after his death. His criticisms of the argument cover several points.

i) An unsound analogy

The strength of the argument depends upon the similarity between the things held to be analogous (that is, the machine and the world). The greater the similarity, the stronger is the argument; the weaker the similarity, the weaker is the argument. But, said Hume, the two analogies are far apart. Our world is *not* like a machine at all since it is composed of vegetables and animals. It is more organic than it is mechanical.

Neither is it philosophically sound to argue that intelligence is the necessary governing principle behind the world. Hume pointed out that there were lots of alternative governing principles (generation, vegetation, gravity). Why should one of these not be the dominant principle? Indeed, why should different principles not rule over their own natural domains: vegetation in plants, generation in animals, gravity in movements of planets? We cannot project from one limited area to another part or to the whole of nature.

Hume re-emphasised the point that the world did *not* closely resemble something man-made by referring to a house; if we see a house we conclude with certainty that it had an architect or builder because we have seen it being built – but the universe does not bear such a resemblance that with certainty we could infer a similar cause (that is, intelligence, thought). Also a number of people are involved in designing a house so perhaps, by analogy, there is a team of gods who designed the world.

ii) Similar effects do not necessarily imply similar causes

Following on from the above points about the lack of similarities between a machine and the world, Hume goes further by questioning whether it is a sound notion that similar effects result necessarily from similar causes. To know that an orderly universe must arise from intelligence and thought, we would have to have experienced the origin of the world. Why should not similar effects be the result of *different* causes?

iii) Other possible analogies

This has already been hinted at in i) above. Hume argued that 'the world plainly resembles more an animal or a vegetable than it does a watch or a knitting loom'. In particular he argued that the world could be compared to a carrot. The relevance of this is that if the analogy is made with the carrot then the mark of design in the world could be caused by something similar to generation or vegetation. The natural world may possess some inner self-regulation and growth. Had Hume lived long enough he may well have quoted **Darwinism** as a possible example. This sees beneficial adaptations explained in non-personal terms by means of natural selection.

Indeed, Hume argued that at its base, intelligence is itself caused by the process of generation! Surely the process of causes continues since intelligence requires a cause. Hence you end up with an infinite regression of causes.

iv) Analogy makes God more human than divine

The more you press the analogy of the man-made machine (for example, a watch) with the universe, the more human you have to make God (similar effects implies similar causes). For instance:

- Infinity could not be attributed to any of the attributes of God. For, as the cause ought only to be proportional to the effect, and the effect is not infinite, so neither have we any reason to ascribe infinity to God.
- Likewise perfection cannot be ascribed. It is impossible for us to tell whether this system contains any great faults. Even if it were perfect, it would remain uncertain whether all the excellences can be ascribed to the workmen. For instance, many worlds might have been botched and bungled before this system was made.
- Hume drove his point home by suggesting the following:

Key question

Do similar effects imply similar causes?

Key thought

There is a difference between God as Creator and God as designer.

Key word

Darwinism: the theory of natural selection to account for changes in nature.

Key question

Is God like a human?

This world is very faulty and imperfect, and was only the first rude essay of some infant deity who afterwards abandoned it, ashamed of his lame performance; it is the work only of some inferior deity and is the object of derision to his superiors; it is the production of old age in some superannuated deity, and ever since his death has run on from the first impulse and active force which he gave it …

v) Analogy leads to a non-moral God

Key question

Is God moral?

Hume listed some unpleasant features of nature, for example, earthquakes, war, disease, and questioned how the planning and design could be that of a just and good God. Workmen have to be judged in proportion to the quality of the work produced! Equally Hume argued that you cannot attribute to the cause anything more than is sufficient to produce the effect. He claimed that a more plausible hypothesis was that of a God who had no moral character. Alternatively there could be two forces, one good and one evil.

vi) Other explanations for apparent order

Key question

Are there other explanations for apparent order?

Hume suggested that we cannot be sure that the so-called organised universe is not the result of some blind, cosmic accident. Indeed any universe is bound to have the appearance of design. There could be no universe at all if the parts of it were not mutually adapted to some degree.

5 Further criticisms

Other arguments against the teleological argument include the following.

Key quotes

'… Darwin made it possible to be an intellectually fulfilled atheist.'
DAWKINS

'Nature red in tooth and claw.'
MILL

- Darwinism, with its appeal for explanation in natural selection, dealt a severe blow to the teleological argument. Darwin demonstrated that order was not necessarily evidence of purpose and design. Order could result from blind chance.
- Mill highlighted the occurrence of disorder in the universe, a criticism that Hume had identified earlier. Milll argued that in nature various atrocities occur that go unpunished. He concluded from this that such things could not result from an intelligent designer who had the attributes of the Christian God. The work of nature is destructive and random. This could not be the work of a benevolent, moral God.
- The debate begins with 'this world' and concludes with concepts of which we have no experience, for example, infinite, uncaused.
- A recent development in linguistic philosophy (see page 144) has centred on the issue of whether statements are meaningful. One conclusion is that a meaningful statement is one where we know what would disprove it. Hence AJ Ayer argued that:

Key quote

'... until we can say what the world would have to be like, to be not designed, we cannot conclude that the world is designed.'

AJ AYER

the world is designed is a meaningless statement [since] until we can say what the world would have to be like, to be not designed, we cannot conclude that the world is designed.

In a similar way, it could be argued that any world, whatever its form, will appear consistent with the idea of a designed universe.

- It has been argued that there is no need to think of things in the universe operating in the light of any kind of purpose. Rather they can be said to come about not in order that something may be achieved, but only as a result of what has already occurred.
- Unless the universe was an orderly place, people would not be around to comment on the fact. Hence there is nothing surprising in the fact that people find order. They couldn't find anything else. Swinburne has responded to this criticism by using his illustration of the card-shuffling machine (*The Existence of God*, 1979, p. 138). He comments:

Key quote

'Maybe only if order is there can we know what is there, but that makes what is there no less extraordinary and in need of explanation.'

SWINBURNE

> *The teleologist's starting point is not that we perceive order rather than disorder, but that order rather than disorder is there. Maybe only if order is there can we know what is there, but that makes what is there no less extraordinary and in need of explanation.*

- We have no certain reason to believe that the universe will continue to behave in an orderly way.

6 Conclusions

Key question

Is the teleological argument persuasive?

Most scholars concede that Hume made some valid points against the argument from design, and in particular about the analogy approach. Certainly in its deductive form it fails, but many find it persuasive as an inductive argument. Kant, though regarding the argument as invalid, stated in his *Critique of Pure Reason* (1781):

> *This proof always deserves to be mentioned with respect. It is the most accordant with the common reason of mankind.*

Despite the general acceptance of some form of the evolutionary theory, many feel it does not eliminate God. This is because the old notion of external design has been replaced by inner self-regulation; and this, in turn, is seen as God's design. In other words, evolution is seen as the means by which God achieves his purpose. In a similar way some argue that evolution is guided by God at key stages, so making sure it reaches the desired end. Supporters of these views are known as 'theistic evolutionists', seeing no contradiction between God as designer and evolution. Still others argue that evolution is not proven and that God remains the designer of the universe. Appeals to recent scientific findings have, for some, drawn attention to the complexities of nature and led them to conclude

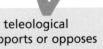

Key quote

'… far from being the "terminus" of the quest for intelligibility and explanation in the universe, God is the terminal illness of reason.'

PETER ATKINS

that the most reasonable explanation is God, whilst for others (for example, Richard Dawkins and Peter Atkins), it has revealed that random changes can lead to order and complex systems can be self-arranging. The debate seems not to have lost any of its vigour.

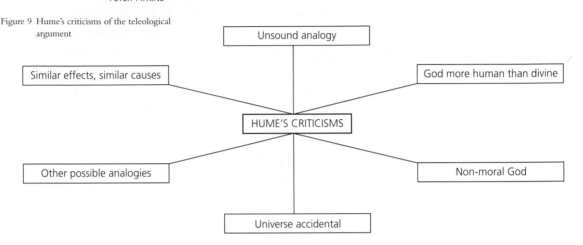

Figure 9 Hume's criticisms of the teleological argument

Study guide

By the end of this chapter you should know and understand the various forms of the teleological argument, especially by Aquinas and Paley, as well as the form based on the anthropic argument. You should know and understand the main weaknesses of the arguments and be able to explain clearly how they weaken the argument. Some responses to those criticisms should also be known.

Revision checklist

Can you name **five** scholars connected with the teleological arguments, and can you state whether each supports or opposes the argument?

Can you explain how each of the following words/phrases is connected to the teleological argument?

- Anthropic
- Cosmological constants
- Analogy
- Irreducible complexity.

Do you know the difference between the following?

- Argument from design–argument to design
- Spatial order–temporal order
- Darwinism–theistic evolution.

Can you give **two** arguments for and against for the following questions?

- Is the teleological argument proof of God's existence?
- Does the teleological argument have more strengths than weaknesses?

Example of exam question

1 Design and the working out of an underlying purpose are evident in the world. The only reasonable explanation for this is that there is a designer and that designer is God.

a) 'Design and the working out of an underlying purpose are evident in the world.' What is the evidence on which this claim is based?

b) Assess the claim that 'The only reasonable explanation for this is that there is a designer and that designer is God.'

Lower level answers will rehearse the various design arguments with little regard for the focus of the question. Higher level candidates will discuss claimed examples of order and regularity. In addition, they will explain the evidence of an underlying purpose such as the anthropic principle. Part b) is testing the AO2 skill. Lower level answers will probably list the criticisms of Hume and state an appropriate conclusion. The listing of material, even if it is a number of criticisms, does not constitute an evaluation or assessment of a claim or view. Evaluation is about a process of reasoning and higher level answers will involve weighing up and responding to criticisms of views. Good answers will question the conclusion that there is a single designer, that the designer still exists. Top level candidates might be expected to debate what constitutes a reasonable explanation. How reasonable is God as an explanation?

Further questions to consider

1 a) Outline the key characteristics of the design argument.
  b) Explain the challenges to the design argument and assess how successful they are.

2 a) Outline the design argument for the existence of God, as presented by Paley.
  b) Explain how science has challenged the design argument.

> ## Chapter checklist
>
> This chapter covers various forms of the moral argument for the existence of God. The basis of most of the arguments is the need to explain the common experience of moral consciousness and obligation. Kant's particular form of the moral argument is also discussed. The criticisms of these arguments are considered, as is the extent to which the arguments can be considered a proof for God.

1 The moral argument

Key word

Moral: relating to human behaviour and what ought and ought not be done.

This argument seeks to show that in the existence of God we find the best solution to the common human experience of moral consciousness and obligation. As with all the theistic proofs, there are various forms of the **moral** argument. They fall into four approaches:

- Aquinas and the fourth of his Five Ways.
- Our conscience and sense of obligation only make sense if there is a divine lawgiver who has sovereign claims.
- If there is no God, there seems no reason to be moral.
- God is required for morality to achieve its end, according to Kant.

a) Aquinas' form of the moral argument

Some people have used Aquinas' fourth 'way' as an entry to the moral argument, though Aquinas does not specifically refer to morality as such. He said that we experience things in the world which are **noble**, true, good and valuable. These things must take their reality from things which are more true, noble, good and valuable. To avoid an infinite regression, there must be something which is the most true, noble, good and valuable. This is what we call 'God'.

By noble, Aquinas seems to mean the quality whereby something is valuable in itself rather than as a means to some other good thing. The argument tries to show that there is something which is the

Key word

Noble: the quality whereby something is valuable in itself rather than as a means to some other good thing.

Key word

Aristotelian: relating to Aristotle or his philosophy.

Key question

What is the explanation for our sense of moral obligation?

Key quote

'If, as is the case, we feel responsibility, are ashamed, are frightened, at transgressing the voice of conscience, this implies that there is One to whom we are responsible, before whom we are ashamed, whose claim upon us we fear.'

JOHN NEWMAN

Key people

John Newman (1801–90) was originally a Church of England priest who converted to Roman Catholicism and became a cardinal.

Key word

Cultural relativism: the acts which are designated right and wrong differ from one culture to another.

cause in every being of its goodness and every other possible perfection. It is a mixture of Platonic and **Aristotelian** ideas, which understood each substance to be a self-contained teleological (goal-orientated) system. The goal to which all things are striving must actually exist. That pure actuality is what we call God.

b) The moral argument from the nature of moral experience

There seem to be a number of human experiences concerning moral consciousness and moral obligation that require explanation. For many, the only satisfactory explanation is the existence of a God.

- There seems to be a universal experience that there is a right and wrong. Certainly all cultures do not agree about *what* is right and wrong but they all appeal to some moral authority which is more than just pragmatism.
- Rightness and wrongness have meaning independently of our judgement of them. That is, they seem to be objective values and do not depend on what we believe or do not believe about them.
- A popular form of this approach sees conscience as the voice of the lawgiver (God). John Newman wrote in his *Grammar of Assent* (1870):

> *If, as is the case, we feel responsibility, are ashamed, are frightened, at transgressing the voice of conscience, this implies that there is One to whom we are responsible, before whom we are ashamed, whose claim upon us we fear. (p. 83)*

Obedience and guilt are only seen to be meaningful if there is a person to whom responsibility is due.

- In a similar way, it is argued that laws imply a lawgiver. There are objectively binding moral laws which can only be explained by the existence of a moral God. Moral claims are best explained in terms of a personal God, given the personal source of ordinary claims and commands. Once we perceive something to be right, we can no longer view it neutrally. There is a pressure on us to respond.

The main criticism to this approach questions the assumption that there are objectively binding moral laws. In other words, our sense of conscience and obligation could be accounted for *without* appealing to the existence of God. Alternative possible explanations include the following.

- **Cultural relativism** – Every society approves and disapproves of particular actions, and teaches its young to think of such actions as 'right' or 'wrong'. Which acts are designated right or wrong differs from one culture to another. Thus morality is a product of

Key people

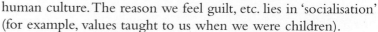

Sigmund Freud (1856–1939) was the founder of psychoanalysis. He claimed that belief in God is an illusion created by humans to resolve their psychological needs.

Key word

Emotivism: claiming that an act is right or wrong is expressing an emotion or attitude, not a fact.

human culture. The reason we feel guilt, etc. lies in 'socialisation' (for example, values taught to us when we were children).

- Subconscious conflicts – Freud saw socialisation as the basis of our morality. He claimed that the origins of conscience could be explained in terms of our psychological development and how we resolved the conflict between our subconscious primitive desires and the demands of society.
- **Emotivism** – When a person states that an act is wrong they are not stating a fact, but merely expressing their own emotion or attitude about the act, in other words, something is 'good' if I approve of it and 'bad' if I do not.
- Evolution – Human beings who had the notion to be kind, helpful, etc. were more likely to survive in the process of natural selection. This characteristic then became genetically transmitted.

This form of the moral argument rests on the assumption that no adequate account can be given for a person's sense of moral obligation. It is certainly contestable whether this assumption is true. For example, unjust societies are a threat to their members, who have good reason to be just if they want to survive and enjoy the many benefits that we know to be possible only in a just society. Hence God's existence is no longer necessary as the source of authority and ultimate sanction.

Even if the moral law requires a source of authority and sanction, that does not mean that there is a source or sanction. What I require to be the case hardly brings the case into reality!

c) The moral argument from idea of ultimate sanctions

Key question

Why behave in a good way if there is no God?

To deny that God exists is to deny the source of authority for good moral behaviour and to deny the ultimate sanction against evil behaviour. Therefore, there would be no reason to behave in a good way. Hence there would be no reason not to act according to our own whims. John Hick points out in *Arguments for the Existence of God* (1970) that, on humanist presuppositions, it would be inconsistent to praise self-sacrifice for the sake of the human community since 'it is unreasonable for anything to be of more value to a man than his own existence'. In other words, it becomes very difficult to justify such heroic acts if God does not exist.

Figure 10 For and against the moral argument

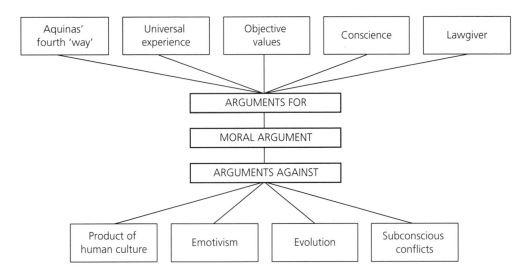

2 Kant's arguments

a) Kant's categories

Kant's moral argument is an example of what he means by the postulate of practical reason. He wants to show that God's existence is implied by man's moral experience. To understand the argument, one has to understand something about the thinking of Kant. He argued that the mind determines the way in which we experience things, rather than the external things in themselves. All we know comes from sense experiences organised by our minds. We cannot know 'things in themselves', but only things as we perceive them to be.

Kant held that the 'categories' by which we understand the world – categories like space, time and causality – were *not* derived from experience. Rather the mind imposes categories on all its experiences (for example, we cannot prove anything has a cause; we assume it and confirm by experience). Thus Kant argued that we cannot prove that we ought to do something by analysing it, since we will never have enough evidence. For Kant, the idea of moral obligation comes from within ourselves – and we experience it as the **categorical imperative**.

Being moral was a case of following this categorical imperative. A genuinely moral action would be one that was done on the maxim which we could will to be a universal law. Thus an immoral action would be one whose underlying maxim could not be intelligibly willed to be universal law (for example, lying to suit my own ends would not be wise for a universal law).

Key word

Categorical imperative: an imperative such as 'Do x' is categorical when it disregards wishes and desires. For Kant, the categorical imperative was the principle that one should act on a maxim only if one can will that it becomes a universal law.

This is the test for good and bad actions. Reason, not feelings, is the guide, and good acts are obligatory because they are rational.

Immanuel Kant (1724–1804)

Kant is often regarded as one of the greatest philosophers of the **Enlightenment**. He argued that we are not entitled to make claims based on human reason about what is not phenomenally accessible, since they are unknowable to us. He therefore thought that the traditional attempts to prove God's existence failed. However, he saw that the idea of God was necessary if the moral world was to be intelligible. Kant argued that the idea of God can only be proved through the moral law and only with practical intent, that is, 'the intent so as to act *as if* there be a God'.

Key words

Enlightenment: an eighteenth-century philosophical movement that stressed the importance of reason.

Summum bonum: the highest good, which comprises virtue and happiness.

b) God is required for morality to achieve its end

The argument for God can be presented by the following steps:

- Our moral experience shows that we are under an obligation to achieve goodness or virtue, and not merely an 'average' level of morality but the highest standard possible. (We recognise an obligation to achieve what is best – real virtue.)
- Beyond this, we recognise also that true virtue should be rewarded by happiness, for it would not be a rationally satisfying state of affairs if happiness came to the unvirtuous or unhappiness to the virtuous. If people were virtuous but were also in pain and misery, their virtue would still be valuable but, nevertheless, the total situation would not be the best possible.
- The desired state of affairs in which man is both virtuous and happy is called by Kant the *summum bonum* (highest good). This we recognise to be what ought to happen.
- Now, in Kant's famous argument, 'ought' implies 'can', that is, an obligation to achieve something implies the possibility that the goal can be achieved (otherwise there can be no obligation). It has to be possible, therefore, for the *summum bonum* to be achieved.
- However, while humans can achieve virtue, it is clearly outside their power to ensure that virtue is rewarded or coincides with happiness.
- Thus there is a need to postulate the existence of God as the one who has the power to bring virtue and happiness into harmony. Such proportioning clearly does not take place before death, so Kant also argued that there must be survival after death.

Note that Kant was not arguing that morality is invalid if God's existence is denied. For Kant, the fact that it is a duty or obligation is sufficient reason to do it. However, he thought that God was demanded if the goal of morality was to be realised.

c) Criticisms of Kant's arguments

Criticisms include such points as:

- Kant argued that 'ought implies can'. If he meant that it was logically possible to bring about the *summum bonum*, then all he was saying was that it was not a logical contradiction. But just because it is not a logical contradiction does not therefore mean that it factually happens. If he meant that it factually happens, we can ask the questions 'Why must it? How can anyone know?' In other words, we question his assumption.
- Why make the assumption that only God can bring about the highest good? 'Why not a pantheon of angels?' suggests Brian Davies (*An Introduction to the Philosophy of Religion*, 1982, p. 96).
- Why make the assumption that virtue must be rewarded with happiness?
- Sense of duty can be explained by other means, for example, socialisation.

d) Conclusions

Therefore, though the arguments fail, they do highlight the point that the rational moral agent 'must believe that a moral reality lies behind the natural order' (C Stephen Evans, *Thinking about Faith*, 1985). In a similar way, Stephen T Davis sees the key issue as being whether 'it is possible to give a compelling account of morality in purely naturalistic terms' (*God, Reason and Theistic Proofs*, 1997).

Figure 11 Kant's arguments

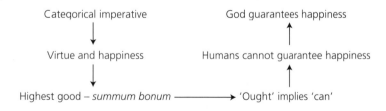

Study guide

By the end of this chapter you should know and understand the various forms of the moral argument, especially Kant's argument. You should know and understand the main weaknesses of the arguments and be able to explain clearly how they weaken the argument. Some responses to those criticisms should also be known.

Revision checklist ✓

Can you name **four** scholars connected with the moral arguments, and can you state whether each supports or opposes the argument?

Can you explain how each of the following words/phrases is connected to the moral argument?

- Moral obligation
- Ultimate sanction
- *Summum bonum*
- Categorical imperative.

Do you know the difference between the following?

- Moral obligation–moral consciousness
- Categories–categorical imperative
- Cultural relativism–socialisation.

Can you give **two** arguments on each side on the following issues?

- Is the moral argument proof of God's existence?
- Does the moral argument have more strengths than weaknesses?

Example of exam question

The moral argument does not prove that God exists, but it does make it probable that God exists. Discuss this assertion.

Lower level answers will tend just to rehearse the arguments without any clear focus on the assertion. The higher level answers will reason through the arguments in terms of proof and probability. The difference between the two terms (proof and probability) may well be explained in terms of inductive and deductive arguments. Good candidates will relate this back to the form of the moral argument and show evidence of a clear process of reasoning.

Further questions to consider

1 There is no relationship between morality and religion. Discuss.

2 Examine Kant's argument for God based on morality. To what extent do its strengths outweigh its weaknesses?

THE EXISTENCE OF GOD – 5 THE RELIGIOUS EXPERIENCE ARGUMENT

Chapter checklist

This chapter covers the argument for God's existence from religious experience. The key differences between 'religious' and 'ordinary' experiences are examined, as are the three main types of religious experience. The question of the authenticity of a religious experience is then discussed, examining some of the difficulties of deciding whether a religious experience is genuine. Finally Swinburne's principle of credulity and principle of testimony are discussed.

1 The religious experience argument

Key word

Monotheism: the belief that there is only one God.

This argument has featured in Western philosophy where the concept of God has been classical **monotheism**.

a) Inductive argument

The design argument looks at features of the universe and infers that the best way to account for them is an appeal to the existence of a God. One form of the religious experience argument works in a similar way. It considers subjective accounts of experiences that have a particular characteristic, and then, like the design argument, infers that they can only be adequately explained in terms of divine agency – God.

The logical form can be expressed in various ways using premises and a conclusion, for example:

- If an entity is experienced then it must exist.
- People claim they experience God.

Therefore God probably exists.

This form of argument is an inductive argument. Remember that in an inductive argument the conclusion may follow from the premises but it does not necessarily follow. Hence this argument can never be considered a proof but may be persuasive.

Richard Swinburne (*Is There a God?*, 1996) points out that it is reasonable to believe that God would seek to interact with his creatures and he gives a list of examples such as God telling us things individually to provide us with a vocation or to authenticate a revelation which we need. God loves us and so may simply show himself to particular individuals. However, many might regard alternative explanations to these experiences as more probable than concluding that such an entity as God exists.

b) Direct awareness of God

This approach does not focus on a reasoned argument – in fact it has no actual argument at all. Experience gives a direct way of knowing about things, distinct from the indirect, inferential way provided by reasoning. Perceiving Victoria Station is the best way of knowing it exists.

This form of argument rests on the view that belief in God is reasonable, not because its truth is entailed by the conclusion of a series of premises, but because God can somehow be directly encountered or immediately perceived. In philosophical jargon this is called a **foundational** or **basic belief**, in the sense that such beliefs are not derived from any other belief. An example of an agreed foundational, basic belief is 'I am in pain.' I know it is true, not by reasoning from other beliefs, but by direct experience.

Alston (*Perceiving God*, 1991) drew attention to the fact that in reports of religious experience, God is experienced as having various qualities, for example, good, powerful or loving. As a result some doubt has been cast on whether it is correct to describe these as foundational beliefs. Is it not necessary for some inference to have taken place to arrive at such conclusions about God?

Everitt in *The Non-existence of God* (2003) gives an example to clarify this view:

> *I look at Fred and thereby acquire the belief that Fred is good. How is this belief to be justified? On the assumption that I am not actually witnessing Fred do or say anything which is good, the justification must surely refer (a) to Fred's visible appearance, and (b) to some correlation between people having that sort of appearance and their being good. In other words, the justification of the belief requires some inference. (p. 154)*

Key word

Foundational (basic) beliefs: a belief that is not derived from any other belief.

2 Differences between 'religious' and 'ordinary' experiences

Key people

Sir Alister Hardy (1896–1985) was a marine biologist with an interest in spiritual phenomena. He set up the Religious Experience Research Unit.

In 1969, Sir Alister Hardy set up the Religious Experience Research Unit (RERU) in Oxford, with the object of examining the extent and nature of the religious experiences of people in Britain. The unit was later moved to the University of Wales,

Lampeter in 2000 and renamed the Alister Hardy Research Centre, in honour of his work.

Part of this research was published by David Hay (*Inner Space*, 1987) and revealed that 25–45 per cent of the population of Britain had been aware of a presence or power beyond themselves. From questionnaires and interviews, the responses about religious experience indicate that:

> *The experience has always been quite different from any other type of experience they have ever had ... and usually induces in the person concerned a conviction that the everyday world is not the whole of reality; there is another dimension to life ... awareness of its presence affects the person's view of the world, it alters behaviour and changes attitudes.*

Key question

What are the differences between 'religious' and 'ordinary' experiences?

Among the differences between 'religious' and 'ordinary' experiences are:

- Religious experiences are wholly other from what is customary and usual.
- God is experienced as opposed to everyday physical objects. A person experiences a spiritual change that clearly has a religious dimension (for example, a person has a new desire to pray and read the Bible).
- It is not usual to be able to describe the religious experience adequately because it is so unlike anything else. We do not have suitable words in our vocabulary.
- The religious experience is not universal to human beings (that is, we do not all have religious experiences but we all experience a tree, etc.).
- Human beings basically use the same conceptual scheme when they describe an ordinary experience. Regardless of culture we all describe a tree in the same way. However, with religious experience, though the feeling may be similar (for example, awe), the object is different (Jesus, Shiva, Muhammad). In other words, religious experiences have different interpretations in different cultures.
- Often a religious experience is a **subjective** experience in a religious experience, whereas an ordinary experience is **objective** (that is, the religious experience often has its source within the mind, whilst ordinary experiences have their source external to the mind and so actually exist).
- Religious experience cannot generally be checked, whereas an ordinary experience is open to checking (for example, it can be seen by others).
- Religious experience gives insight into the unseen whereas the ordinary gives no insight into other realms.

Key words

Subjective: having its source within the mind.

Objective: external to the mind, actually existing.

- God cannot be experienced unless He allows it. In contrast, an ordinary experience may be experienced by anyone in the right place at the right time with the requisite sense organs.

3 Types of religious experience

Religious experiences have been described across religions and through the centuries. Some are spontaneous whilst others are the result of training and discipline, but they all share the common feature of an awareness of the divine. This awareness can take the form of:

- A sense of oneness or union with the divine.
- A sense of dependence on the divine.
- A sense of separateness from the divine.

Clearly any experience may contain more than one of these elements.

A definition of 'religious experience' could be 'an experience that has religious insight'. This insight is usually into the unseen dimensions of existence and may well affect the outlook and behaviour of the recipient of the experience. They realise that the everyday world is not the whole of reality.

Recently, Swinburne (*The Existence of God*, 1979) has centred on religious experience as a key argument for God's existence. He identifies five types of religious experience in which a person seems to perceive God:

- Experiencing a perfectly normal non-religious object or event, for example, a night sky. The night sky is not God, but God is encountered through it. The object or event is seen as the handiwork of God, a sign from God, an address by God or that which points to God.
- Experiencing a very unusual public object, for example, the resurrection appearances of Jesus or the appearance of the Virgin Mary at Lourdes.

These first two are both public events in that, in theory, people present could have seen what was happening and experienced God through the event. The last three are private.

- Experiencing private sensations that are describable by normal vocabulary, for example, Joseph's dream of the angel.
- Experiencing private sensations that are not describable by normal vocabulary, for example, a mystical experience such as those of St Teresa of Avila (see page 66).
- Non-sensory experience. The person would be unable to refer to anything in particular that made it seem they were experiencing God. 'It just did!'

a) Mysticism

A mystical experience is the name given to the experience of having apprehended an ultimate reality that is difficult to express using normal vocabulary. It characteristically involves some kind of sense of the unity of all things in one substance and one life. There are numerous ways of classifying the experiences. For instance, Stace (*Mysticism and Philosophy*, 1960) distinguished between an extrovertive (outward-looking) and an introvertive (inward-looking) mystical experience. Jonathan Webber (*Revelation and Religious Experience*, 1995) summarises the difference between the two as follows:

> *The extrovertive is one where the plurality of objects in the world are transfigured into a single living entity. In contrast, the introvertive mystic speaks of losing their identity as a separate individual and slowly merging into the divine unity.*

Webber gives an example of an introvertive mystic experience which comes from the Chandogya Upanishads:

> *As rivers flow to their rest in the ocean and there leave behind them name and form, so the knower, liberated from name and form, reaches that divine Person beyond the beyond.*

Others distinguish between 'theistic mysticism' and 'monistic mysticism'. The latter involves an awareness of the soul, selfhood or consciousness rather than God. However, the classic account of mysticism is given by William James (*The Varieties of Religious Experience*, 1902) who lists, with examples, four main characteristics of mystic experiences:

- **Ineffability** They are states of feeling so unlike anything else that it is not possible to import or transfer them to others. They defy expression. Descriptions such as 'the dissolution of the personal ego' and 'the sense of peace and sacredness' are empty phrases to those who have not experienced such things.
- **Noetic** quality Though ineffable, the mystic experience produces states of insight into truths unobtainable by the intellect alone. They are revelations. They are not trivial. They are universal and eternal truths.
- **Transiency** The religious experience does not last for long, usually half an hour or so. Though they are remembered, they are imperfectly recalled, but recognised if they recur. If a series of mystic experiences take place, then usually there is some sort of development of inner richness. They usually leave the recipient with a profound sense of the importance of the experience.
- **Passivity** Mystical states can be helped by such things as 'fixing the attention' or 'going through certain bodily movements', but

Key word

Mysticism: the experience of having apprehended an ultimate reality.

Key quote

'... as a lump of salt cast in water would dissolve right into the water ... Arising out of these elements (bhuta), into them also one vanishes away ...'
BRHADARANYAKA, *UPANISHAD* II.2

Key people

William James (1842–1910) was probably the first person to carry out major research into religious experience. He came to it from a background of psychology.

Key words

Ineffable: indescribable, cannot be expressed in words.

Noetic: relating to the mind.

Transiency: not permanent. Lasting for short time only.

Passivity: not active, not participating in the activity.

when the state occurs, the mystic feels as if they are taken over by a superior power. This can result in phenomena that suggest alternative personality states – for example, prophetic speech, speaking in tongues.

One of the classic mystics connected to Christian tradition is St Teresa of Avila. In her writings, the ineffable characteristic is prevalent, for example, in *The Collected Works of St Teresa of Avila* (1987):

> the soul is fully awake as regards God, but wholly asleep as regards things of this world … God establishes himself in the interior of this soul in such a way that when I return to myself, it is wholly impossible for me to doubt that I have been in God, and God in me.

Associated with Teresa's 'raptures' are always visions. Her most famous vision involved her seeing a small angel with a beautiful face holding 'a long golden spear', tipped with a 'little fire', which he thrust into her heart. She says:

> … it penetrated into my entrails. When he drew out the spear he seemed to be drawing them out with it, leaving me all on fire with a wondrous love for God.

William James gives a list of examples that range from those that have no special religious significance (for example, 'I've heard that said all my life, but never realised its full meaning until now') to those that are intensely religious.

Most mystical experiences occur when in a conscious state and the person differentiates between that experience and a dream. William James reports the following example:

> There came upon me a sense of immense exultation and joyousness followed by an intellectual illumination impossible to describe. Among other things, I did not merely come to believe, but I saw that the universe is not composed of dead matter but rather a living Presence; I became conscious in myself of eternal life … The vision lasted a few seconds and was gone but the memory of it and the sense of reality of what it taught have remained … I knew that what the vision showed me was true.

Another approach to analysing some mystical experiences is by reference to the numinous. This term is often used to describe the experience in which God's separateness is highlighted. It was coined by Rudolf Otto in his book *The Idea of the Holy* (1917). The word comes from the Latin *numen*, meaning divinity.

For Otto, religion sprang from experience of the holy. However, because this word had so many associations, he used *numen*. It is something that is 'wholly other' than the natural world. He analysed this type of experience in terms of the Latin phrase *mysterium*

Key people

St Teresa of Avila (1515–82) was a Spanish mystic and monastic reformer.

Key quote

'God establishes himself in the interior of this soul in such a way that when I return to myself, it is wholly impossible for me to doubt that I have been in God, and God in me.'

ST TERESA OF AVILA

Key word

Numen: something that is 'wholly other' than the natural world.

Key people

Rudolph Otto (1869–1937) coined the term 'numinous' in his book *The Idea of the Holy* (1917).

tremendum et fascinans. Ninian Smart explains this as 'a mystery which is awe-inspiring and fascinating and points towards the Transcendent'. People are drawn towards it, hoping for holiness, yet also realising that there is but One Being who is holy.

In his book, Otto illustrates this type of experience by examples from a variety of religions. This emphasis on the 'otherness' of God tends to put an impersonal idea at the heart of religion.

In contrast, Martin Buber stresses personal relationships and that which underlies them. In his book *I and Thou* (1937), Buber argues for two kinds of relationships: the I–It and the I–Thou. The former is when we view people and things as merely phenomena. By probing deeper we can enter the second relationship both with people and things, such that we can call it a personal relationship.

> *It is here that we encounter a Thou over against our I. And this is the realm also where we encounter God.*

This approach is interpreted as an experience of God through our relationships with people and the world.

b) Conversion

Conversion denotes the changing from one set of beliefs to another. In religious terms a person can convert from one faith to another: from being an atheist to being a theist; from being a believer to being a non-believer. Conversion can be a sudden process or a gradual one. Often it involves feelings of guilt (a conviction of 'sin'), a search for faith, sometimes voices but usually at least some sort of divine communication, and a resulting assurance or feeling of certainty.

Possibly the best-known example is that of Saul (later called St Paul) who had a conversion experience on his way to Damascus, where he had intended to persecute some Christians (see Acts 9:1–18). Paul's conversion was not putting on a patch of holiness *but* rather it was holiness woven into all his power, principles and practice. He described himself as a new man, a new creation.

Another well-known example is that of John Wesley. He was aware that he did not have the faith in Christ as a personal saviour that he saw others had. However, on 24 May 1738, at a meeting of an evangelical society in Aldersgate, London, he had a conversion experience. He wrote in his journal for that day:

> *I felt my heart strangely warmed. I felt I did trust in Christ, Christ alone, for salvation; and an assurance was given me, that He had taken away my sins, even mine ...*

Wesley is a good example of conversion from faith (believing) to faith (trusting). It was a movement from academic acceptance to personal trust.

Key people

Martin Buber (1878–1965) was a Jewish philosopher who examined how one could relate through dialogue with the uniquely Other (I–Thou) rather than as subject to object (I–It).

Key word

Conversion: the changing from one set of beliefs to another.

Key people

John Wesley (1703–91) was the founder of the Methodist movement.

Key quote

'I felt my heart strangely warmed.'
WESLEY

Examples of gradual conversion usually involve the building up, piece by piece, of a new set of beliefs and habits. However, even this type of conversion often has critical points at which the movement forward seems much more rapid. One of the characteristics of this gradual conversion is a voluntary and conscious act by the person.

William James concludes by noting that the persons who have passed through conversion, having once taken a stand for the religious life, tend to feel themselves identified with it, no matter how much their religious enthusiasm declines.

c) Prayer

The wide sense of the word **prayer** includes every kind of inward communion or conversation with the power recognised as divine. Using Christianity as an example, seven different types can be identified that occur in the Bible:

- blessing (Ephesians 1:3)
- adoration (Psalm 95:6)
- petition (Colossians 4:12)
- asking forgiveness (Luke 18:13)
- intercession (1 Timothy 2:1)
- thanksgiving (1 Thessalonians 5:18)
- praise (Ephesians 3:20).

In a sense all religious experience is about prayer, that is, communion with God. Prayer in this wide sense is the very essence of religion. Indeed, it is prayer that distinguishes the religious phenomenon from other phenomena such as the purely moral. Prayer is the conviction that something is genuinely transacted, that things that cannot be realised in any other way come about.

William James uses the example of George Muller of Bristol, who died in 1898. He was well known for running orphanages and schools and lived by prayer, believing that God provides. His custom was never to run up bills, not even for a week. He also made it a point never to tell people of his needs. His biography relates the vast number of times that, for instance, there was no food to feed the children in the orphanage, and then it would be provided by someone.

Many religious people claim that through a prayerful life they experience 'coincidences' that make it seem that their life is guided.

In Christianity, one of the focuses of the Pentecostal churches has been on speaking in tongues, particularly when praying. Speaking in tongues is claimed to be the New Testament phenomenon where a person or persons speak in a language that is unknown to them. The Pentecostal experience may be defined as seeking and receiving the gift of speaking in tongues as a sign of the Baptism of the Holy Spirit. Kildahl (*The Psychology of Speaking in Tongues*, 1972) gives an example of how speaking in tongues (**glossolalia**) can be initiated:

Key quote
'I finally ceased to resist, and gave myself up, though it was a hard struggle. Gradually the feeling came over me that I had done my part, and God was willing to do his.'
CITED BY WILLIAM JAMES

Key word
Prayer: inward communication with the divine.

Key quote
'Now to him who is able to do immeasurably more than all we ask or imagine, according to his power that is at work within us, to him be glory ...'
EPHESIANS 3:20

Key quote
'When I pray, coincidences happen, and when I don't, they don't.'
WILLIAM TEMPLE

Key word
Glossolalia: speaking in tongues, that is, speaking in an unknown language.

Typically after an ordinary evening church service, interested members of the congregation are invited to remain in church in order to discuss the gift of tongues. The leader encourages the people to 'receive' this ability, going from one another laying his hands on each person's head. 'Say after me what I say, and then go on speaking in the tongue that the Lord will give you.' One might utter a few syllables, speak for two or three minutes, or ten, or not for several days and while at home. 'It was the best I ever felt in all my thirty-one years.' … Once possessed of this ability, a person retains it and can speak with fluency whenever they choose. It is referred to as a 'direct and personal encounter with the Holy Spirit'. (p. 2f)

Key questions

Are the claims of the charismatic movement true?

Is glossolalia the work of the Holy Spirit?

Within Christianity, many traditionalists are uneasy about some of the claims of the charismatic movement to such religious experience. Some challenge it on theological grounds, claiming that the gift of tongues was only given in the Early Church times and then ceased. Others challenge on grounds that what we see being exhibited today is not the same as speaking in tongues in the New Testament, and that natural explanations can explain today's phenomenon. It has been claimed that glossolalia has a specific language structure based on the language tongue of the speaker; that the linguistic organisation is limited; and that the capacity to speak in this type of semi-organised language can be duplicated under experimental conditions. Thus, on this view, glossolalia does not appear to be a 'strange language', but rather the aborted or incomplete formation of familiar language. In contrast, others claim it is the work of the Holy Spirit, reviving and equipping the Church with a new outpouring of the Spirit.

(For further discussion see the Religious Experience book in the Access series.)

Figure 12 Types of religious experience

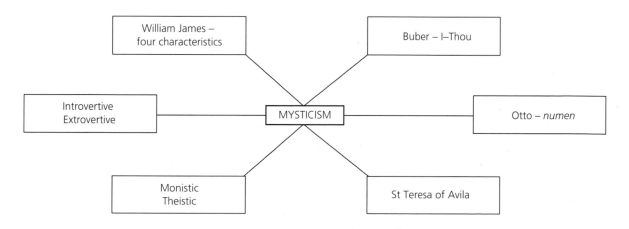

Figure 12 Types of religious experience *continued on p. 70*

Figure 12 Types of religious experience *continued*

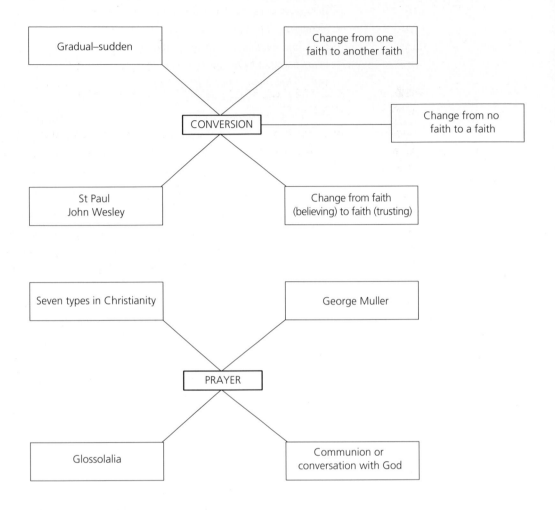

4 Is a religious experience authentic?

As has been noted above, a religious experience cannot be authenticated in the way that an ordinary sense experience can be. Religious experiences are very much a private matter rather than a public one, and it is not possible therefore to check someone else's religious experience. If the event is a public one, then it still entails a religious interpretation. Even more problematic is the private event.

A number of points have been discussed about this whole area.

a) Is an 'experience of God' a philosophically sound notion?

When people try to describe an experience of God, they tend to make comparisons that raise problems philosophically. Analogies

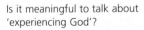

Key question

Is it meaningful to talk about 'experiencing God'?

are appealed to, to justify the philosophical notion of a religious experience of God, but many argue that the analogies have weaknesses:

- 'It is like a sense experience.' People argue that just as you can encounter a table, you can also encounter God, but the two are very different. For instance, God is not material, nor does He have a definite location. Also, claims of encounters with objects can be checked, but when the object is God, they are not verifiable.
- 'It is similar to an experience of people.' People argue that just as we are known to each other by a kind of direct apprehension rather than through our physical body, so in the same way we experience God who is non-corporeal.

Key question

Is experiencing God similar to experiencing a person?

First, this assumes that people are non-corporeal (that is, dualistic in nature). Second, even if people are mind and body, we still encounter them when they have bodies. Knowing they are there involves knowing that their bodies exist. In contrast, God has no body at all. Therefore an encounter with God is radically different from an encounter with a person. Third, we are aware of how many people we are having an encounter with (that is, they are physical units distinguishable in some way from others), because it involves reference to material factors. However, when we encounter God, He is not material yet is said to be one being. Finally, there are theological reasons to question the idea that God can be known in the same way as we can know a person. According to the Bible, God is not a person, for example, 'God is Love'.

Can God be recognised?

Key question

How would you know that it was God that you were experiencing?

The problem arises as to how you can distinguish God from other possible objects of experience. For instance, God is said to be the Creator. How would you recognise that attribute? God is said also to be omnipresent, infinite, omnipotent and eternal. But how, simply by virtue of an awareness of an object of experience, can anything be recognised to be that? To recognise omniscience, you would have to be omniscient yourself!

One solution is to argue that an experience of God would be a self-authenticating experience. But feelings of certainty can occur when in fact I am wrong. Just declaring that 'You know' is insufficient. There must be reasons as well as convictions.

Direct experience of God is impossible

Key question

Is every experience inferred and interpreted?

Some claim that the finite cannot experience the infinite — so we cannot experience God. Others argue that to speak of a direct experience is not philosophically correct since we infer and interpret every experience. For instance, even an ordinary object is mediated and interpreted via our sense data and organs.

Indeed, it could be argued that the religious person interprets experience according to a religious framework of life, whilst the atheist interprets it as purely natural events. Hick referred to this as 'experiencing-as' and illustrated it using the ambiguous figure of the 'rabbit–duck'.

b) Is there is a natural explanation?

When we speak of an experience, there are two distinct elements: that which is experienced (**objective**) and my experience of what is experienced (**subjective**). Many people question the objective, claiming that there is no religious reality, only the person's wrong interpretation of the source of the experience. Hence, various other sources are offered and the following points made.

- Experience is often deceptive – hallucinations, for example. However, mistakes do not demand that all experiences are therefore in error. It is true that we may regard a particular witness as unreliable, but for the argument to be valid, all people who claim experience would have to be known to be unreliable. Clearly such a position is difficult to maintain.
- The psychological may be taken into account – for instance, conversion may meet the psychological needs of people. Freud saw religious experience as a reaction to a hostile world. We feel helpless and seek a father figure, thus we create a God who is able to satisfy our needs. Jung suggested the archetype deep within us. Sexual frustration is said to be the explanation of St Teresa of Avila's mystic experiences, especially the one involving the spear! Appeal is made to recent research that includes the link between certain personality types and religious interest, as well as talk of identifying a 'religious gene'.

However, even if people need a father figure, it does not mean that God is not like that. There does still remain the possibility that such a state is a necessary requirement for the experience, but such a state would not necessarily negate acclaimed experience of God.

c) Reasons that make it unlikely

Some people feel that there is an inconsistency about the argument, that if it were true then surely certain things would be expected to follow, for example, the experience should be fairly uniform.

i) There is no God, therefore the experience of God cannot be valid

This is an a priori conviction, whose reasons would need to be examined. This has gained strength in recent times with the debate about whether God is really an object/being. Some reject the traditional understanding of the word 'God' and see it more as 'a form of life' which the believer inhabits. It is a way of expressing a particular way of looking at the world and does not refer to any external, objective being. For further discussion on this approach see chapter 14 on religious language.

ii) Lack of uniformity of experience

The fact that different experiences are recounted does not mean that they are therefore all in error. Also this explanation implies that the different experiences are logically incompatible, which is not necessarily true. The lack of uniformity may also be due to the interpretation rather than the falsity of the actual religious experience.

iii) Not all experience it

Surely if there was a God, He would want everyone to know about Him and therefore all should have religious experiences. However, it could be argued that some precondition, like faith, is required. Also the initiative may have to come from God, who may be selective. Alternatively, perhaps He does reveal himself but we are unable to see it (like a tone-deaf person unable to appreciate music). Indeed, believers assume often that others can have the experience and even encourage them to do so (for example, evangelism).

d) Reasons that may make it likely

Religious experience is not a conclusive argument for the existence of God. One may believe that what is experienced is actually God, but there is always the possibility that others may interpret it differently.

Whether religious experience is seen to be caused by God will depend to a great extent upon individual presuppositions. If one's presuppositions favour particular types of experiences, one is likely to be convinced of reports of them.

However, it is not proof because it does not compel you to conclude that God exists, but criteria may be applied that would add weight to the validity of the religious experience:

- It must be in keeping with the character of God as made known in different ways, for example, through natural theology, agreement with doctrine and resemblance of experience to classic cases in religious tradition as judged by spiritual authorities.
- The results of the experience should make a noticeable difference to the religious life of the person. It should lead to a new life marked by virtues such as wisdom, humility and goodness of life. It should build up the community rather than destroy it. St Teresa of Avila said:

> *Though the devil can give some pleasures – only God-produced experiences leave the soul in peace and tranquillity and devotion to God.*

Key question

If people experienced God, wouldn't the experiences all be similar?

Key question

Why would God choose to show himself to some but not to others? Surely this would be unfair?

Key question

Are there any criteria that if applied, would add weight to the validity of the religious experience?

● The person should be regarded as someone who is mentally and psychologically well-balanced.

Wainwright (*Philosophy of Religion*, 1988) comments that the only conclusive grounds for rejecting religious experiences would be:

● Proofs of the non-existence of God and other supernatural entities.
● Good reasons for thinking that the perceptual claims immediately based on these experiences are inconsistent.
● Evidence that the experiences are produced by natural mechanisms known to systematically cause false beliefs and delusive experiences.

Wainwright's personal conclusion is that, so far, critics have not provided these grounds. For a very different conclusion read chapter 10 in Mackie's book *The Miracle of Theism* (1982).

e) The principle of credulity and the principle of testimony

Richard Swinburne has given much importance to the argument from religious experience (*The Existence of God*, 1979), as does Caroline Franks Davis' book *The Evidential Force of Religious Experience* (1989). In particular, Swinburne puts forward two principles.

The principle of credulity

Key people

Richard Swinburne (b 1934) is an Oxford professor who has devoted himself to promoting arguments for theism.

Swinburne's argument is focused on the onus of proof and put in the context of ordinary sense experiences. He argued that we are justified in accepting an event occurs unless there are strong reasons to the contrary, for example, grounds for supposing the viewer was hallucinating! It is up to the disbeliever to show that it is unreasonable to believe the account, rather than for the believer to show that it is reasonable to believe. In other words, it is a case of religious experiences being viewed as true until proven otherwise.

Key question

Is it up to the disbeliever to show that it is unreasonable to believe, or up to the believer to show that it is reasonable to believe?

To express this principle formally: 'In the absence of any special considerations, if it seems that X is present to a person, then probably X is present.' What one seems to perceive is probably the case. Swinburne points out that unless we do this we cannot know anything. We would have to be sceptical about all our sense experiences. If my experience of seeing a cat in a tree does not justify my belief that there is a cat in the tree – then it seems that I could never be justified in believing that there is a cat in the tree. Nor indeed anything else for that matter.

He then lists four considerations that, if present, would cast doubt on the reliability of the account:

● if subject 'S' was unreliable
● if similar perceptions are shown to be false

- if there is no strong evidence that X was not present
- if X can be accounted for in other ways.

Key question

Do Swinburne's four considerations cast doubt on the reliability of a religious experience account?

However, he feels that these four considerations do not weigh against religious experience. For example:

- if the person is known to be a liar – but this does not account for all cases.
- if the experience itself was made under circumstances that have proved unreliable in the past – for example, if the person is under the influence of LSD. Again does not account for all cases!
- given God is everywhere, the opposer according to Swinburne would need to show that God did not exist. This they have not done.
- can be accounted for in other ways – but to find the causal chain in my brain, such as for example the temporal lobes, does not show that it is unreliable. God is everywhere and sustains all causal processes, therefore He can use normal means to communicate with me!

Key question

What would convince you that a person had a religious experience?

If you want to read a full account of this, then see chapter 13 in Swinburne's book *The Existence of God*.

The principle of testimony

Swinburne argues that, in the absence of special considerations, it is reasonable to believe that the experiences of others are probably as they report them. In other words, we should believe other people unless we have good reason not to. Clearly he accepts the point that people can lie or be mistaken, but the significance of this approach is to put the onus on the sceptic to show that religious experience should be rejected rather than for the believer to show that it is true. This approach may not show that any religious experiences are veridical, but equally it does show that they could be. This is particularly important as a cumulative argument if all the other arguments for the existence of God are evenly balanced.

f) In conclusion

Key question

Does the origin of a religious experience have to be religious?

It should be noted that some argue that the origin of an experience is irrelevant. The fact that the source may be an ordinary experience does not mean that the experience cannot become a religious one by the interpretation of the subject.

Figure 13 The religious experience argument

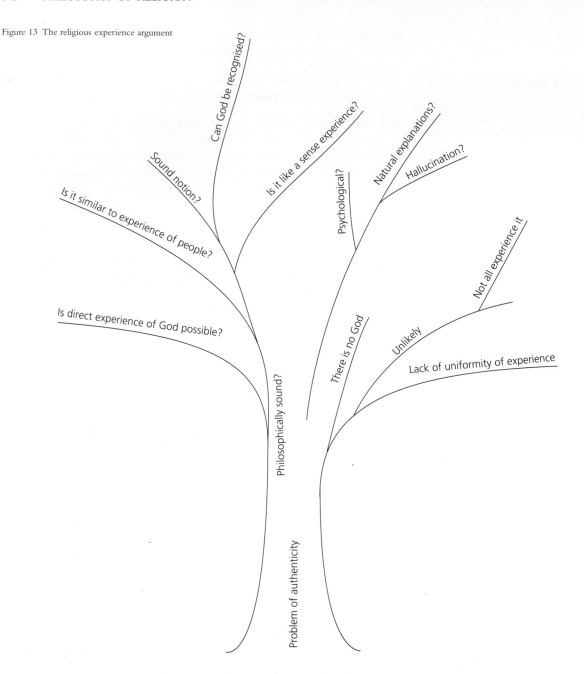

Can God be recognised?

Sound notion?

Is it like a sense experience?

Natural explanations?

Hallucination?

Is it similar to experience of people?

Psychological?

Not all experience it

Is direct experience of God possible?

There is no God

Unlikely

Lack of uniformity of experience

Philosophically sound?

Problem of authenticity

Study guide

By the end of this chapter you should know and understand the argument from religious experience for the existence of God. You should be able to explain the differences between ordinary and religious experiences, as well as discuss and illustrate the three main types of religious experience. Finally you should be able to assess the main difficulties in deciding an experience is a genuine religious experience.

Revision checklist

Can you list and illustrate **five** differences between ordinary and religious experiences?

Can you list and explain the **four** main characteristics of mystic experiences?

Can you explain how each of the following could be seen as a problem for authenticating religious experiences?

- Religious experiences differ.
- Not everyone has a religious experience.
- God is experienced.

Do you know the difference between the following?

- Principle of credulity–principle of testimony
- Objective–subjective
- Mysticism–prayer
- Introvertive–extrovertive
- Monistic–theistic.

Can you give **two** arguments on each side on the following issues?

- Is the religious experience argument proof of God's existence?
- Does the religious experience argument have more strengths than weaknesses?

Example of exam question

To what extent can religious experience be viewed as a reasonable argument for the existence of God?

There are various forms of the religious experience argument for God's existence. It is acceptable either to centre on one or to cover a broader range in a less detailed way. Lower level candidates will tend to drift into writing about religious types of experience. Higher level answers will be focused on the slant of the question. There will also be some appropriate use of philosophical terminology, as well as some key thinkers, such as Swinburne.

Lower level answers will be descriptive rather than contain evidence of a process of reasoning (AO2). In particular, the higher level answers will discuss the idea of 'reasonableness'. Reasonableness often involves risking a hypothesis as true in the light of other competing statements, as well as weighing up the probability of the evidence. However, the failure to find a more probable competing hypothesis does not prove that there is none. Equally, there remains the difficulty over how we individually weigh up what is more probable. This is usually affected by our presuppositions.

Further questions to consider

1 a) What are the distinctive features of a 'mystical' experience?
  b) Consider the view that calling an experience 'mystical' is doing no more than giving an ordinary experience a religious interpretation. Evaluate this claim.

2 a) Describe the main features of (i) mysticism and (ii) conversion experience.
  b) To what extent does religious experience prove God's existence?

MIRACLES

1 What is a miracle?

The previous chapters have considered the evidence for God based on inference from the existence and nature of the universe. However, if there is a God who is perfectly good and loving, then it may be expected that He will not only sustain the universe minute by minute but also on occasions intervene in His creation in special ways. These special occasions are often referred to as miracles and constitute a further argument for the existence of God. Whereas the earlier arguments focused on familiar and normal experiences, this argument focuses on events so rare and unusual that they are seen as signs of divine activity.

a) Miracles as interventions

This classic understanding of 'a miracle' focuses on the interventionist approach. A miracle involves some intervention by God such that without that intervention, the event would not have taken place. The intervention is usually seen in terms of the breaking of a **law of nature**. Aquinas defined miracles, saying, 'Those things must properly be called miraculous which are done by divine power apart from the order generally followed in things.' He was one of the earliest philosophers to attempt to define a miracle, and distinguished between three kinds of miracles:

Key word

Law of nature: a generalisation based on regular happenings within nature.

- Events in which something is done by God that nature could never do, for example, the sun going back on its course across the sky.
- Events in which God does something that nature can do, but not in this order, for example, someone living after death.
- Events that occur when God does what is usually

Lourdes

done by the working of nature, but without the operation of the principles of nature, for example, someone instantly cured of an illness that usually takes much longer to cure.

Probably the best-known expression of this understanding of miracles is by David Hume, who defined a miracle as:

A transgression of a law of nature by a particular volition of the Deity or by the interposition of some invisible agent. (Enquiry concerning Human Understanding, 1777)

However, two problem areas arise that may undermine the coherency of such a definition. One problem concerns the phrase 'laws of nature', whilst the other focuses on the nature of God. A coherent definition is one that makes sense and is logically consistent.

i) Laws of nature

Does it make sense to say that a law of nature has been broken? The problem arises because of our understanding of laws of nature. If laws of nature are generalisations formulated retrospectively to cover what has happened, then there cannot be miracles. For whenever any event happens that is outside of the established natural laws, it would simply mean that we must widen the law to cover this new case. In other words, supposed laws of nature that are broken are better described as incomplete laws that need widening to incorporate the new happening. For instance, the natural scientist would argue that there is no reason for thinking that a particular law of nature has been supernaturally overridden: it's simply that the original law was wrong and now has to be adapted to include the new happening.

Is it coherent to talk about laws of nature at all? If nature is to some extent random as modern science may suggest, then we can never know whether some law has been broken or whether things are happening in a natural but random way as opposed to a natural but ordered way.

Key quote

'A miracle is a transgression of a law of nature by a particular volition of the Deity or by the interposition of some invisible agent.'

HUME

Key questions

Is the definition of miracle coherent?

Can a law of nature be broken?

Key question

How would you know a law of nature had been broken?

Alistair McKinnon argues that laws of nature are simply 'whatever occurs'. In his article 'Miracle and Paradox', in *American Philosophical Quarterly* 4 (1967), he says that laws of nature are:

> simply highly generalised shorthand descriptions of how things do in fact happen … Hence there can be no suspensions of natural law rightly understood. Miracle contains a contradiction … if for natural law we substitute the expression the actual course of events … Miracle would then be defined as an event involving the suspension of the actual course of events.

Hume's phrase 'transgressing a law of nature' seems inappropriate. Laws of nature merely describe what will occur given a particular set of initial conditions. When those conditions are changed in some way, then the 'law' does not apply. When a miracle occurs, the initial conditions are different, since God's special activity is now also a new added condition. Hence the 'law' has not been transgressed.

ii) Nature of God

To say that God intervenes in the working of the universe seems to imply a view of God as spectator of events. It suggests that an agent moves in where He had not been before. This is contrary to **classical theism** where God is seen as sustainer and preserver of the universe.

If God is considered to be outside of time, then maybe it is incoherent to believe that a timeless God enters time and space and acts, since at that moment He would be limited to a time frame.

b) Miracles as having religious significance

Many think miracles need to hold some deeper religious significance than just breaking laws of nature. Richard Swinburne in *The Concept of Miracle* (1970) argued:

> If a god intervened in the natural order to make a feather land here rather than there for no deep ultimate purpose, or to upset a child's box of toys just for spite, these events would not naturally be described as miracles.

Certainly the Judaeo-Christian tradition supports this understanding where miracles are seen as signs from God. The word 'sign' is used in John's Gospel to refer to Jesus' miracles that always seem to point to something beyond the actual event. The Gospel miracles were not seen as an end in themselves (compare Luke 10:13). However, the acceptance that God can intervene and that God is good does raise questions about the problem of evil and of a moral God. If God is all good and all powerful, then why are there so few miracles? Why doesn't God address the problems of the world more directly by means of miracles? What are we to make of a God who stands by and watches, as millions of people are led to gas chambers, yet who seemingly intervenes to heal an individual? Surely such a God would not be worthy of worship. Maurice Wiles expressed this tension in his book *God's Action in the World* (1986):

Key question

Is God sustainer or spectator?

Key word

Classical theism: traditional Western belief about the nature and attributes of God.

Key quotes

'If a god intervened in the natural order to make a feather land here rather than there for no deep ultimate purpose … these events would not naturally be described as miracles.'

SWINBURNE

'Woe to you Korazin … For if the miracles that were performed in you had been performed in Tyre and Sidon, they would have repented long ago …'

LUKE 10:13

Key people

Maurice Wiles (1923–2005)
rejected the possibility that God directly intervenes in the world and therefore rejected the existence of miracles. He argued that either God acts arbitrarily (and is therefore not worthy of worship) or that He does not intervene at all.

Miracles must by definition be relatively infrequent or else the whole idea of laws of nature … would be undermined, and ordered life as we know it would be an impossibility. Yet even so it would seem strange that no miraculous intervention prevented Auschwitz or Hiroshima, while the purposes apparently forwarded by some of the miracles acclaimed in traditional Christian faith seem trivial by comparison.

A God who acts in such a trivial way is, according to Wiles, a God not worthy of worship. This implies miracles do not happen if belief in a traditional God is to be maintained. However, this depends on prior beliefs about the nature of God. If there is other evidence that God is all-loving, then God may have reasons for acting as He does. For further discussion see chapter 11.

c) Miracles as interpretations

Ray Holland presents a completely different point of view on defining miracles. His most often quoted illustration is of the boy in a toy car caught between the railway tracks with a train fast approaching and out of sight. The mother could see both the boy on the tracks and the train approaching. The train suddenly started to slow down even though the driver could not see the boy ahead. The train eventually stopped about a metre away from the boy, therefore leaving him unharmed. The mother looking on saw it as a miracle. She still said it was a miracle, even when she was later told that the reason for the train stopping was that the driver had had a heavy meal, suffered a heart attack and passed out, causing the automatic braking system to come into play and so stop the train.

Key question

Can an event that has an explanation within natural law be called a miracle?

Holland claimed that an event that has explanation within natural laws nevertheless can be considered a miracle if it is taken religiously as a sign. Holland refers to this as a 'contingency miracle'. The presence of religious significance is sufficient, according to Holland, for a certain event to be termed a miracle. Reading Holland's account ('The Miraculous', *American Philosophical Quarterly* 2, 1965), it is not clear whether he was arguing that God actually intervened. On balance it seems that Holland wants us to think that it was divine providence that the driver fainted at that particular moment. William Craig ('Creation, Providence and Miracles?', in B Davies [ed.], *Philosophy of Religion: A Guide to the Subject*, 1998) discusses how theologians have identified different types of divine providence, in particular the type that Holland may be expressing in his toy car illustration:

As Paul and Silas lie bound in prison for preaching the gospel, an earthquake occurs, springing the prison doors and unfastening their fetters … God can providentially order the world so that the natural causes of such events are, as it were, ready and waiting to produce such events at the propitious time, perhaps in answer to prayers which God knew would be offered. (p. 152)

Anti-realism: truth is relative to the community who are making the statement.

Enlightenment: an eighteenth-century philosophical movement that stressed the importance of reason.

Key people

Rudolf Bultmann (1884–1976) was a theologian who denied that there could be miracles. He reinterpreted the supernatural elements of the gospels (demythologising).

Others read into Holland's illustration a more **anti-realist** understanding. For an anti-realist, a miraculous event is an event that is a disclosure. It is not about a real action that a supernatural being has undertaken. It is an interpretation of an ordinary event. The event makes sense within the form of life of the religious believer and involves no 'real' actions of a God. This approach had already been aired from the time of the **Enlightenment**. Whereas biblical scholars such as Reimarus (1694–1768) had argued that the Gospel writers had distorted the accounts about Jesus, or gave the miracles natural explanations (Jesus walking on a sandbank not on water), Strauss (1808–74) introduced the idea of 'myth'. He did not challenge the Gospel writers' integrity but interpreted miracles in the light of first-century Palestinian culture, which Strauss saw as dominated by a mythical world view. He did not regard miracles as actual historical events. Bultmann developed this view, arguing that the mythological world view portrayed in the New Testament was unintelligible and unacceptable. As far as miracles were concerned, they needed to be reinterpreted and their spiritual truths made clear.

There have, of course, been criticisms of this approach. Apart from its dismissal of the historical reliability of the Gospel accounts, this understanding of miracles is far removed from the more traditional definition demanding intervention by a supernatural God. Holland's approach can be seen as very subjective, since it relies on the viewer interpreting and labelling the event as 'miraculous'. It is not objective. It is a very personal assessment where an event has to be classed as miraculous if someone believes it to be so. Their naming it as a miracle makes it, by definition, a miracle. Those who criticise this approach are not necessarily denying that interpretation is important. They are claiming that miracles, if they happen, must have an objective reality.

Figure 14 Definitions of miracle

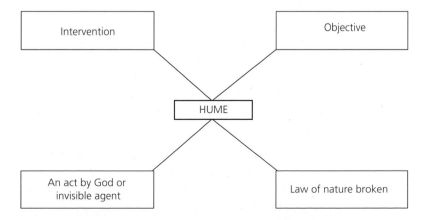

Figure 14 Definitions of miracle *continued*

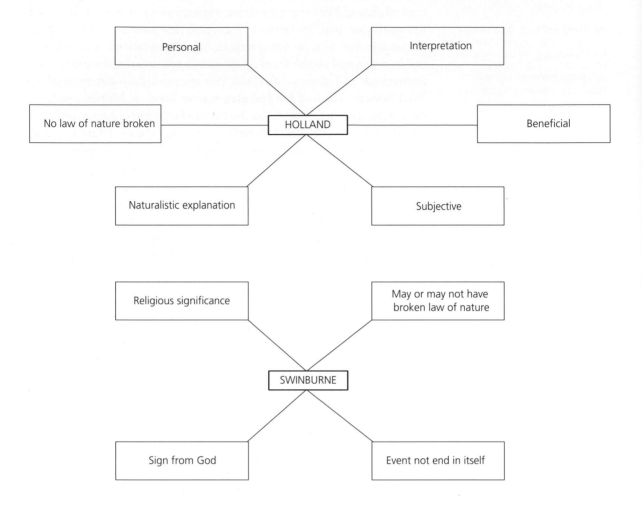

2 Is it reasonable to believe in miracles?

The answer to this question depends on what definition we are accepting. If we accept Holland's interpretative understanding of miracles, then they occur whenever anyone so interprets an event as such. Most philosophical debate has centred on the more traditional understanding of miracles, particularly expressed by Hume. Although Hume's chapter on miracles in his book *Enquiry concerning Human Understanding* (1777) is scarcely twenty pages long, it is regarded as a major contribution to the debate.

a) Hume and the importance of testimony

David Hume wrote his famous chapter on miracles to demonstrate that no one could prove with certainty that a miracle had occurred. This served the purpose of undermining the use of miracles to demonstrate the truth of Christianity in particular, and religion in general. He did not deny the possibility of miracles since this would be contrary to the **empiricist** position, which was the basis of all his philosophy. As an empiricist he believed that all questions of truth had to be based on experience, which therefore involves an enquiry about evidence. Given that a wise person 'proportions' their belief to the evidence, and that laws of nature have been established and supported over a period of many hundreds of years, then it will always be more reasonable to believe that the law of nature has held and has not been broken, than to believe testimony claiming that the law of nature has been broken. In particular he noted that there were no equivalents in modern-day events that compared to the recorded miraculous events in the Bible. Hence he focused on testimony of others in the distant past. He concluded (*Enquiry concerning Human Understanding*) that their testimony could never outweigh our present-day experience of the regularity of nature:

> *No testimony is sufficient to establish a miracle unless the testimony be of such a kind that its falsehood would be more miraculous than the fact which it endeavours to establish.*

In particular, he highlighted several reasons why testimony was less likely to be true. He argued that a miraculous event has never been proven to be true because:

- *No miracle has a sufficient number of witnesses.* What is required is a quantity of educated trustworthy witnesses to a public event – people who would have a lot to lose if found to be lying.
- *People are prone to look for marvels and wonders.* We all like ghost stories and recount them even when we don't believe them.
- *The source of miracle stories are from ignorant peoples.* This seems to be partly referring to uneducated Galilean peasants, for example, in the Gospels. The miracle stories acquired authority without critical or rational inquiry.
- *The writers had a vested interest and so there was bias.* This was particularly the case if a miracle was being used to establish a religion (for example, the Resurrection).
- *Religious traditions counteract each other.* This last argument is different from the other four. Unreliability here does not derive from the unreliability of the witnesses; rather, that the evidence is further contradicted by other witnesses. If an Islamic miracle supports Islam and so discredits Christianity as a true religion, then equally any claim of a Christian miracle will likewise discredit Islam. Hence, evidence for one is evidence against the other and vice versa. This seems to undermine the evidence.

Hence Hume's conclusion that it was more rational to distrust the testimony about a miracle than to believe that the law of nature had

Key word

Empiricist: one who believes that all knowledge derives from experience.

Key question

Is testimony reliable and trustworthy?

been broken. Indeed some commentators would argue that Hume thought miracles were impossible. For a discussion on whether this is a fair conclusion see M Palmer, *The Question of God* (2001), pp. 182-83.

b) Responses to Hume

A number of responses have been made in reply to Hume's argument.

i) Hume and his empiricism

Key question

Are religious people biased?

Hume argued that for an event to be counted as a miracle it must violate the uniform experience that makes up the law of nature. He also claimed that all the empirical evidence relevant to the law had confirmed it as having no exceptions. This seems to beg the question that surely one cannot say nature has been uniform unless the assumption is made that all miracles are false. Further, if it is argued that exceptions to law cannot be sufficient to overthrow the law, but rather the exception is unreliable – then how do laws ever change? Logically we should never accept an exception! And therefore never change a law!

David Hume (1711–77)

PROFILE

A Scottish philosopher and empiricist, Hume claimed that knowledge was based on sensory impressions and since there can be no sensory impressions of God, there can therefore be no knowledge about God. Hume regarded religion as operating outside of reason and was therefore very critical. He rejected the possibility of miraculous happenings. It is unclear whether he was an atheist.

ii) Probability

Key word

Naturalism: an account of the world in terms of natural causes and natural forces.

Hume seems to equate probability with 'frequency of event'. By their very nature one would not expect many miracles. If **naturalism**, as opposed to supernaturalism, is assumed, then miracles will be rejected. Those who are theists will be more inclined to see miracles as likely to have happened, since it would be consistent with their beliefs. For them it has little to do with 'how many' but more to do with God's nature and purposes. Wise people should base their beliefs on facts, rather than odds.

iii) The criteria for testimony

Key question

Did Hume believe miracles were impossible or just that there had not yet been adequate evidence for one?

Many regard Hume's criteria for testimony as being too stringent. If applied consistently to all past occurrences, might we not have to give up the writing of history?

It is questionable whether Hume would ever have accepted any testimony for a miracle. He goes on to refer to instances of 'miracles' in France which supposedly took place during his lifetime. These were 'immediately proved on the spot, before judges of unquestioned integrity, attested by witnesses of credit and distinction, in a learned age in a cultured country'. Hume refused to credit such testimony on the grounds of 'the absolute impossibility or miraculous nature of the events which they relate' (*Enquiry concerning Human Understanding*, 1777).

Hume writes as if all believers were either deceivers or the deceived. He fails to take into account the possibility that some people, including religious people, are by nature sceptics.

iv) The self-cancelling argument

The argument that miracles have a self-cancelling nature has been questioned on two counts. First, some advocates of one religion will now often allow that a number of other religions have at least some elements of truth and may even have divine authority. Therefore miracles could occur in other religions. Second, some argue that miracles can be performed by other sources than God (for example, evil forces), and these may be the sources of miracles in some other religions.

Even if Hume were right about the self-cancelling, it would not follow that the evidence for all miracles would be invalidated, for the evidence for the miracles of one religion might be much more impressive than the evidence for miracles in another.

v) Other evidence

Hume was writing at a time when the only support for a miracle came from a testimony. However, today we may be able to appeal to scientific evidence and so on. He did not consider the kinds of physical effects or traces which a miracle might leave, which might provide evidence for its occurrence independent of testimony. For instance, a healed withered leg stands as evidence, apart from the testimony of the one healed, or X-rays, photographs or videotapes.

3 Modern supporters

Amongst the most recent defenders of miracles are the philosopher Richard Swinburne and the physicist/theologian John Polkinghorne. Both argue that science does not prove that miracles are impossible or self-contradictory. In addition, Swinburne (*The Concept of Miracle*, 1970) argues the case that evidence for a non-repeatable happening, which breaks the law of nature, is acceptable historical evidence. This dismisses Hume's claim that the law of nature must always be the stronger evidence. The fact that God is the cause of the extraordinary event is strengthened if the event occurs in answer to a prayer and if it is an act consistent with the nature of God. Swinburne (*The Concept of Miracle*) also attacks the argument that when a law of nature

Key question

Is God the only being able to do miracles?

Key question

Is testimony the only evidence for miracles?

Key people

John Polkinghorne (b 1930)
Professor of Mathematical Physics at Cambridge University until he resigned his chair and became an Anglican priest. He argues that science and religion both address aspects of the same reality.

appears to be broken it is either because we are mistaken or that we are not yet aware of the true law.

> We have to some extent good evidence about what are laws of nature, and some of them are so well established and account for so much data that any modification of them which we could suggest to account for the odd counter instance would be so clumsy and ad hoc as to upset the whole structure of science. (p. 32)

Indeed, it has been said that to salvage the law of nature requires just too many ad hoc adjustments. For example, the law of nature that people die and stay dead may be amended by the clause, 'Except when the person's name begins with the letter J; he claims to be God and founds a major Western religion.' Such an approach for maintaining that laws of nature are never transgressed seems unreasonable.

The thrust of Swinburne's arguments is to show that it is rational to believe that a miracle has occurred, while allowing the possibility that evidence might turn up later to show that we are mistaken. He comments:

> 'We may be mistaken' is a knife which cuts both ways – we may be mistaken in believing that an event is not a divine intervention when really it is, as well as the other way around. (Is There a God?, 1996, p. 121)

Another recent defence of miracles has attacked the anti-realist, demythologising approach to biblical miracles. The book *In Defence of Miracles* (ed. R Geivett, 1997) contains a number of articles arguing the case for the historical reliability of the resurrection of Jesus. Certainly it is true that if you reject the supernatural, then you must reject the miracles as historical events. However, this seems a purely arbitrary decision since many argue that the strongest evidence for the supernatural is found in the Gospel accounts. They would claim that there are very good reasons for accepting the Gospels as historical documents. For example, see Craig Blomberg, *The Historical Reliability of the Gospels* (1987).

4 What might miracles prove?

a) Miracles show that God exists

Miracles have often been viewed as an inductive proof for the existence of God since they are consistent with the existence of God. It is the best explanation of certain irregular states of affairs.

The difficulties of this approach include:

Key quote

'... that He was buried, that He was raised on the third day according to the Scriptures, and that He appeared to Peter, and then to the Twelve. After that, He appeared to more than five hundred of the brothers at the same time, most of whom are still living ...'

1 CORINTHIANS 15: 5–6

Key question

Is it rational to believe that a miracle has happened?

Key quote

'"We may be mistaken" is a knife which cuts both ways – we may be mistaken in believing that an event is not a divine intervention when really it is, as well as the other way around.'

SWINBURNE

- How do we identify an irregular state of affairs?
- How do we justify the introduction of the concept of God to account for such an event?
- Is Hume's understanding of miracles incoherent?

However, the arguments for God's existence can be seen to be part of a cumulative argument (see chapter 9).

b) Miracles can show the authenticity of a revelation

Key question

Should we expect miracles?

Certainly the Judaeo-Christian tradition supports this view. For instance Hebrews 2:3–4:

> *This salvation, which was first announced by the Lord, was confirmed to us by those who heard him. God also testified to it by signs, wonders and various miracles …*

Miracles may function like a divine signature, confirming God's actual sponsorship of a particular revelation claim.

Swinburne argues that we should expect miracles, given that we expect revelation. Since God needs to communicate with His creatures, He needs to authenticate His revelation. God may be considered to exist via other arguments for God. Given that if God exists, miracles are not impossible – then attention focuses on the historical evidence for that miracle occurring.

Criticisms of this approach include challenging:

Key question

Does God need to authenticate his revelation?

- the assumption that God probably exists
- the assumption that God is interested in giving revelation to His creatures
- the assumption that we can be sure about the occurrence of miracles through historical investigation.

c) Miracles reveal the nature of God

Miracles are an essential part of the actual content of the revelation. According to the Christian tradition, Jesus entered our world by means of the Virgin Birth. Jesus died but overcame death. His resurrected body was seen and touched by His disciples. When Jesus walked the earth, He came into conflict with evil and was victorious over it (the exorcisms, etc.). Prophecy is fulfilled. God acts through answering prayer and actively intervenes in and sustains the universe.

The questions raised about this approach include:

Key word

Incarnation: God taking on human form in the person of Jesus.

- Is the historical evidence sufficiently convincing?
- Is the **Incarnation** coherent with the nature of God?
- If Jesus is God, how can He die?
- Why does God intervene so few times and often in such limited situations (the problem of evil)?
- How can a timeless God intervene in time?

Figure 15 Weight of evidence according to Hume

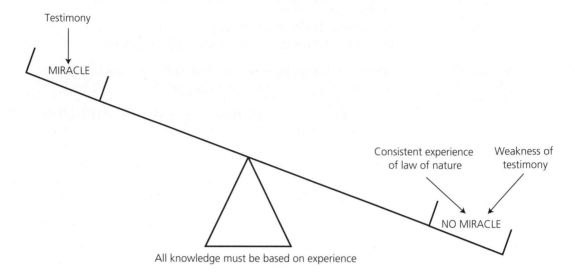

Study guide

By the end of this chapter you should know and understand the different definitions of 'miracle' and be able to critically assess the problems that these different definitions pose. You should also be able to discuss what miracles might prove, if they were authentic.

Revision checklist

Can you state **four** of Hume's arguments against miracles?

Can you state **three** things that miracles might prove?

Can you state and illustrate **three** different definitions of miracles?

Can you explain the ways that the different definitions both resolve and create problems?

Can you give counter-arguments to Hume's arguments against miracles?

Examples of exam questions

1 A miracle is an amazing coincidence of a beneficial nature. A miracle is an event of religious significance.

Explain these two definitions of miracles.

The lower level answer will tell the story of the boy and the train, or some other story, in great detail but omit to explain the point of the illustration. Higher level answers will allude to the illustration avoiding a full, lengthy graphic account, and will draw out the various aspects of the definition, such as subjective interpretation, that the illustrations exemplify. Key thinkers such as Holland and Swinburne would be expected to be referred to in higher level answers.

2 Explain Hume's challenges to belief in miracles and assess how far his criticisms are justified.

The AO1 element involves the explanation of Hume's criticisms. Lower level answers will tend just to list the criticisms without context or explanation. The higher level answers will refer them first to Hume's definition of miracle and then to his context of Hume's empiricist position and the weighing against regular events (laws of nature).

   The AO2 involves assessing the strengths of Hume's position. Again the lower level answers will tend to list responses to Hume's criticisms. This is not really a demonstration of the AO2 skill. Evaluation requires a process of reasoning and arguing a position. Listing data is more akin to AO1 skill.

Further questions to consider

1 'If we accept that violations of natural law do occur, then the conclusion follows that God causes them.' Assess this view.

2 'Miracles do happen.' Explain what a believer might mean by this, referring to at least two definitions of 'miracle' in your answer.

THE VALUE OF THEISTIC PROOFS

1 Cumulative arguments

It is generally agreed that, as deductive arguments (see chapter 1), the theistic proofs fail. However, as has been noted, the recent approach sees them more as probabilities and inductive. In particular, Swinburne argues that 'the probability of theism is none too close to 1 or 0' (*The Existence of God*, 1979, pp. 290–91). In other words, he agrees that they are fairly evenly balanced. He then considers the religious experience argument and sees this as making theism overall probable. Swinburne argues that his conditions have been met as regards his two principles (see chapter 7), and no special considerations hold given that he has shown that the other theistic arguments cannot be classed as 'very improbable'. Hence he concludes that theism is more probable than not.

Certainly this type of cumulative approach has been used by others, though not in the specific form that Swinburne has used. Often appeal is made to the **Occam's razor** approach (alternative spelling is Ockham), which claims that unnecessary entities should be erased (hence 'razor'). Hence the solution to all the questions raised by the theistic arguments such as cause, order and regularity, and morality, is the one entity, called God. This is regarded as a simpler solution since it only requires the single entity 'God' for a solution to *all* the arguments. However, whether the introduction of the entity 'God' is really a simpler answer has been challenged, given

Key word

Occam's razor: the principle that entities should not be multiplied beyond necessity.

Key people

William of Occam (1288–1349) was an English Franciscan friar and scholastic philosopher. The principle of Occam's razor is attributed to him.

the complexities of the concept of God! Also, none of the different arguments for God's existence proves that He is the God of classical theism. Nonetheless, as Davis points out (*God, Reason and Theistic Proofs*, 1997), if the beings proved to exist by the arguments 'are all one and the same being, then clearly we have arrived at the existence of a being that is remarkably similar to the God of theism' (p. 188).

The usual **cumulative argument** takes the form of accepting that though each argument in itself is not a proof, the arguments when added together become more convincing. In other words, theism is the one solution that all the arguments point to and that most satisfactorily takes account of the wide range of data. Various analogies have been used to illustrate this approach. For instance, if you have a leaky bucket (inductive argument for God's existence) and insert other leaky buckets inside it (more arguments for God's existence), then the leaks are sealed (that is, the arguments gain strength)! Others have been quick to point out that $0 + 0 = 0$ (in other words, a failed argument added to another failed argument results in both failing!).

Obviously the persuasiveness of the inductive arguments will depend on each of the separate arguments having some probability. John Hick sees the heart of the issue as a decision as to whether the universe is ultimately intelligible or whether it is a 'brute fact'. To people who believe the former, theism will appear a reasonable explanation.

Key word

Cumulative argument: a collection of arguments that together increase the persuasiveness of the case.

Key questions

Are the arguments for God more convincing when added together?

Is theism a reasonable explanation?

2 Criticisms

Recent writings have seen an increasing attack on the whole idea of theistic proofs. This has come from a number of different angles.

a) Rationality

Richard Messer (*Does God's Existence Need Proof?*, 1997) notes that Swinburne assumes that his logical argument will convince any rational person. The assumption being 'that there is a paradigm standard of rationality to which people should adhere'. Messer suggests that the Wittgensteinian approach of conceptual relativity challenges Swinburne's assumptions. Swinburne is accused of making the judgement that all viewpoints other than his own are inadequate. In other words that the view that he, Swinburne, holds is what does actually constitute reality.

However, many like Wittgenstein would point out that our idea of what constitutes rationality depends on our 'conceptual frameworks and criteria for making judgments' (Messer, p. 121). How we interpret evidence depends on our already existing ideas.

RM Hare coined the term 'blik' to mean a framework within which events are interpreted. (For further discussion about bliks see below and chapter 14.)

Alvin Plantinga is another modern-day philosopher who has challenged our understanding of rationality. He questions the basis of rationality which rests on **foundationalism**. Foundationalism is the view that rational belief must either be supported by evidence or by **basic beliefs**. Basic beliefs are those beliefs that seem so obviously true that we feel compelled to agree with them. Hence, basic beliefs must be either self-evident, incorrigible (cannot be mistaken) or evident to the senses. For example, if I believe I am in pain, then it cannot be false that I am in pain. This is a basic belief that requires no evidence or justification. Applying this understanding of rationality to the issue of a belief in God means that for rational belief in God, some evidence is required by the believer, since the belief does not fulfil the criteria for a basic belief.

Plantinga argues that theistic beliefs can be basic beliefs. He does this by raising two criticisms against foundationalism:

- Believing 'I had lunch yesterday' does not satisfy the basic belief criteria, yet it is a basic belief in that there is no reasoning taking place. I may use reason to repel a belief that my memory is faulty, but my belief is not inferred from my reasons for rejecting the view that my memory is faulty. Hence Plantinga shows that our criteria for basic beliefs are inadequate.
- Foundationalism itself does not meet its own criteria as a basic belief. The belief that 'all rational beliefs must be either basic or justifiable according to basic beliefs' is itself neither a basic belief nor justifiable in terms of basic beliefs. Hence, according to foundationalism, foundationalism itself is irrational.

Plantinga is therefore arguing that we cannot say a priori what the criteria are for a basic belief. Rather we should try to identify common features of the basic beliefs that people have in their thought system. Plantinga maintains that belief in God is one such basic belief since it has the feature of an unfounded belief which provides the foundation for other beliefs. Hence belief in God does not require evidence to justify it, to make it a rational belief. It is a basic belief. A theist's belief in God is as rational as one's memory beliefs. Plantinga regards humans as having a natural capacity to apprehend God's existence on a par with our natural capacity to apprehend truths about the past. For a good critique of Plantinga's position see W Wainwright, *Philosophy of Religion*, 1988, pp. 155–59.

b) Faith and belief

Often a criticism is made along the lines of 'Well, if God was proven, there would be no room for faith.' The implication is that

Key quote

'We walk by faith not by sight.'
2 CORINTHIANS 5:7

such a proof would devalue the importance of faith. Indeed, it is argued that a religious belief cannot be subjected to proof. In support of this view is often quoted a verse from Paul's letter to Corinth: 'We walk by faith not by sight' (2 Corinthians 5:7). Faith is seen as a contrast to knowledge, implying that it is an area that is not totally certain. RM Hare argued that the religious believer does not make assertions that are either true or false but adopts 'bliks'. This is the principle by which we live and with which we interpret experience. Hare used the illustration of an Oxford don who was convinced that all the other Oxford dons were trying to poison him. Any examples of behaviour that suggested differently were seen as a subtle attempt to put him off his guard. Such belief is a 'blik' and nothing can count against it. It cannot be refuted by evidence because it helps to determine what counts as evidence.

This emphasis on faith rather than rational argument reflects the views of the philosopher Kierkegaard. He gave three arguments why reason played no part in faith:

Key people

Søren Kierkegaard (1813–55)
the Danish philosopher and theologian, stressed the action of the will and the choice of faith apart from reason.

- For the believer, faith in God was a statement of a certainty rather than a statement of mere probability. However, reasoning could never produce a certainty and so reasoning has no relevance to faith.
- Authentic faith requires a degree of commitment such that the believers do not imagine they will change their belief or abandon it. Reasoned argument could never produce such a commitment. Kierkegaard saw that what was required was 'a leap of faith', so that the belief would remain even when argument failed.
- Without risk there could be no faith. Indeed 'intense passion' is the essential feature of religious faith. This means that the greater the leap, the better the quality of the faith. Passion, for Kierkegaard, varies in proportion to the risk's enormity. The risk is greatest when faith's object is not just uncertain but absurd. Hence faith in the Incarnation, which Kierkegaard felt reason rejects as absurd.

The view that the central tenets of religions are not able to be shown to be the case by rational argument, but must be accepted on faith, is called **fideism**. Most fideists do not deny that reason has a role in religion (though some do), but claim that faith precedes reason in matters of religion.

Key word

Fideism: the view that certain beliefs are beyond the scope of reason and must be accepted on faith.

Karl Barth is another example of someone who places faith above reason and so rejects the approach that focuses on weighing up the arguments for God. Barth's three main defences of this position are cited by J Webber (*Faith and Reason*, 1995):

Key people

Karl Barth (1886–1968)
rejected any form of philosophy that he thought exalted itself over God's self-revelation.

- God can only be known through Jesus and anyone to whom the Son chooses to reveal Himself.

- Human reason is corrupted as a result of the Fall.
- Divine revelation is the ultimate criterion of truth, not human reason.

Hence 'Christian truths are revealed by God, and anything that is revealed by God is true irrespective of the findings of human reason' (*Faith and Reason*, p. 20). However, problems arise over judging between different religious claims of revelation, and the assumption that there is indeed a God who reveals.

For further discussion on belief/faith and evidence, see the next chapter.

c) Understanding of the word 'God'

Perhaps the strongest attack on theistic proofs has come from the area of philosophy of language. The assumption in the theistic proofs is that 'God' is an external, independent objective being. This is to regard statements about 'God' as **cognitive**. Cognitive statements are statements that are true or false in the ways that literal statements are true or false. However, other philosophers see religious statements as more **non-cognitive** (that is, not open to truth or falsity at all). On this understanding, religious beliefs are not factual claims. A belief in the last judgement has nothing to do with events that will happen in the future; rather, it is reflecting about the meaning of life and death. Messer sums up the issue clearly (*Does God's Existence Need Proof?*) with a quote from DZ Phillips:

> *Coming to see that there is a God is not like coming to see that an additional being exists. If it were, there would be an extension of one's knowledge of facts, but no extension of one's understanding. Coming to see that there is a God involves seeing a new meaning in one's life, and being given a new understanding. (p.51)*

Therefore, the theistic proofs are seen to be irrelevant at best and a total misunderstanding of what 'God exists' means. There is no new fact to discover but rather seeing what is already here in a completely new way. To be an atheist is not about rejecting factual beliefs but more about rejecting a way of life. For further discussion of this approach see chapter 14.

Figure 16 Challenges to arguments for God's existence

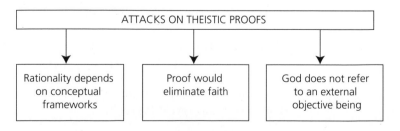

Study guide

By the end of this chapter you should know and understand the cumulative argument for the existence of God and the challenges made against the whole concept of theistic proofs.

Revision checklist

Can you name **five** scholars connected with the theistic proofs, and can you state whether each supports or opposes the idea that God's existence can be argued for?

Can you explain how each of the following words/phrases is connected to theistic proofs?

- Occam's razor
- Blik
- Foundationalism
- Fideism
- Non-cognitive statements.

Can you state the **three** main attacks on the idea of theistic proofs?

Example of exam question

To what extent does Kierkegaard show that faith is opposed to reason?

This is an evaluative question (AO2 skill), and so requires some evidence of reasoning and weighing up of the evidence. Lower level answers will tend to list points rather than integrating them. A good answer will not just state a critique but will also respond to that critique. The discussion about Kierkegaard's three arguments might include:

- Is it true that faith requires certitude?
- Shouldn't religious believers be humble and open to correction?
- Should we believe in Santa Claus, as that requires strong faith?

Further questions to consider

1 'If God was proven, there would be no room for faith.' Discuss.

2 'Theistic proofs are irrelevant in the twenty-first century.' Discuss.

1 Belief

Key question

What is meant by 'belief'?

It is important to understand what is meant by the word 'belief'. In everyday speech, to say 'I believe something is true' is often taken to mean 'I believe that it is probably true.' However, in its more precise sense, the word 'belief' means 'I have a conviction that it is true.' That conviction is not necessarily there as a result of logical argument. Belief may come about by deductive argument, by inductive argument, by personal experience or even by sheer blind personal acceptance and prejudice.

2 Belief-that and belief-in

Key word

Belief-that: a belief that claims to be an objective fact.

First, consider **belief-that**. A typical 'belief-that' statement is 'I believe that the Pope is the head of the Roman Catholic Church.' The statement is making a claim that is objectively true and that something is a fact. We call this propositional belief. A person believes that:

- Some state, process or thing exists independently of the actual belief that they exist.
- This belief is more likely to be true than any rival or alternative belief.
- The likelihood of one statement of belief being true as opposed to another rival statement being untrue lies with:

– the statement is consistent with our general perception of what is true

– the greater or more persuasive evidence for it; and

● The statement is true.

What counts as evidence for the belief will depend on the nature of the statement. The belief that there is a table in the room will be based on the senses. In contrast, historical statements will be evaluated differently. The essential issue is that such evidence indicates that the truth of the belief is more likely than not, and more likely than alternative propositions. These criteria are what we mean when we speak of a rational belief.

In contrast, an irrational belief can be described as a belief:

● for which the person has no evidence whatsoever

● which conflicts with or contradicts, and is known to do so, other well-grounded beliefs that the person holds

● which the person claims to know is false, while continuing to believe it

● for which the person claims there could never be evidence.

Key word

Belief-in: a belief that conveys an attitude of trust or commitment.

Now consider **belief-in** statements. An example of a belief-in statement would be 'I believe in Jesus', where clearly this usually means more than just belief that Jesus was a historical figure. It also implies trust in Jesus. Belief-in may be contrasted with belief-that, by saying belief-in conveys an attitude of commitment, trust or loyalty on the part of the believer This attitude, or psychological stance, forms part of the object of belief-in. It is, however, difficult to see these two as contrasts as it would be irrational to trust or be loyal to something one did not believe to exist.

Ludwig Wittgenstein (1889–1951) held a view of belief that reflected something of the belief-in understanding of commitment and trust. In his *Philosophical Investigations* (1953) he stated:

> *'I believe' is not giving a report on my state of mind. Believing … is a kind of disposition of the believing person … shown … by his behaviour. (II, 191)*

In this view, 'belief' is seen not so much as a mental state, but more as a disposition to respond in certain ways to certain circumstances. For further discussion on Wittgenstein see chapter 14.

3 Belief and evidence

There are some things that are easy to believe, such as 'The Queen lives at Buckingham Palace'. There are some things that are difficult to believe, such as 'The table is made up of atoms that have gaps

Key people

William Clifford (1845–79)
was a mathematician and
philosopher. He argued that it was
immoral to believe things for
which one lacked evidence, and
did not see faith as a virtue.

Key quote

*'It is wrong always, everywhere,
and for anyone, to believe anything
upon insufficient evidence.'*
WILLIAM CLIFFORD

Key word

Blik: a framework within which
events are interpreted. An
unfalsified conviction.

between them'. There are some things that I can't make myself
believe, such as 'The world is flat'. I can't make myself believe that
because the evidence overwhelmingly implies the world is round. In
other words, we hold beliefs because there is some degree of
evidence for that belief.

John Locke (1632–1704) argued that the only opinions that had
a right to be held were those that had evidence to support them.
William Clifford expressed the same view even more forcibly when
he wrote:

> *It is wrong always, everywhere, and for anyone, to believe anything upon
> insufficient evidence. (*Lectures and Essays, *1879)*

For Clifford there was a moral obligation about deciding what to
believe, since poorly supported beliefs could harm other people. He
gave an illustration of a ship owner who, though he had doubts
about the ship's seaworthiness, nevertheless sent sailors to sea in it.
He persuaded himself that the ship would be guarded against
accident. As a result, the sailors died as the ship went down in mid-
ocean. Clifford argues that the man was guilty of the deaths of the
sailors, 'since he has no right to believe on such evidence as was
before him' (*Lectures and Essays*). Equally, if people accepted beliefs
without any evidence, then they would be more likely to believe
wrong things in the future and so harm themselves:

> *Every time we let ourselves believe for unworthy reasons, we weaken
> our powers of self-control, of doubting, of judicially and fairly weighing
> evidence.*

William James (1842–1910) responded to Clifford's views, arguing
that it is right to believe in some cases where there is a lack of
strong supporting evidence. When we are faced with choices that
are 'living, forced and momentous' but lack good objective
evidence, then we make our decisions with our 'passional nature'. In
particular, James sees the religious hypothesis as just such a choice.
For a good discussion on this see Wainwright's *Philosophy of Religion*
(1988), pp. 148–53.

As we saw in the last chapter (p.95), Hare also challenged the role
of reason for religious beliefs. He argued that the religious believer
does not make assertions that are either true or false but adopts **bliks**,
and so nothing can count against the assertion of the religious
believer. However, this is challenged by those who point out that
things do count against a religious belief (that is, there is a weighing
up of evidence, so arguments for God are relevant). For instance, if
there were evidence that Jesus never lived, then one would have no
right to believe that Jesus rose from the dead. Brian Davies (*Thinking
about God*, 1985) makes a number of observations concerning belief
and evidence (pp. 244–60), including the following:

- Not all beliefs are provable. Indeed if we are to believe anything at all, there must be inferred beliefs to start with.
- We are often entitled to belief without proof; for instance, believing things that people say to us if they are experts.
- Certain central beliefs of Christianity illustrate the problem of proof (for example, the doctrine of **Incarnation** that Jesus is both fully human and fully God). One attempted solution has been to appeal to historical accounts of Jesus in the Gospels. However, even if we were to accept the accounts as accurate, 'an interpretation going beyond the evidence would still be required'. The issue is that the doctrine is not just a report of historical facts.
- Though we often use the word 'belief' of things open to doubt, we also use it of things we can prove, that we can give solid evidence for and regard as conclusively proved.

Key word

Incarnation: God taking on human form in the person of Jesus.

4 Faith

When trying to define faith, most thinkers have juggled a mixture of will, propositional belief and trust. Aquinas worked from the premise that the Christian faith was fundamentally rational. As such, it could be supported and explored by reason, as Aquinas demonstrated with his Five Ways (see p. 35). However, for Aquinas, the foundation is divine revelation, since reason alone could not discover the truths and insights of the Christian faith.

A McGrath (*Christian Theology: An Introduction*, 1994) identifies three components to Martin Luther's concept of Christian faith:

Key people

Martin Luther (1483–1546) challenged the sale of indulgences by the Roman Catholic Church and sparked the Protestant Reformation.

- Faith has a personal, rather than a purely historical, reference. Belief in the facts, by themselves, is not adequate for true Christian faith.
- Faith concerns trust in the promises of God. Faith is not just about believing something is true but being prepared to act upon that belief.
- Faith unites the believer to Christ. Faith makes both Christ and his benefits – such as forgiveness, justification, and hope – available to the believer. (p. 129)

As we have seen above, faith seems to include a belief-in, as well as a belief-that. Hence personal trust is often seen as an important element. An act of the will is used in deciding and abiding by that choice. Luther (cited by McGrath, *Christian Theology*, p. 127) used the illustration of a boat:

The person who does not have faith is like someone who has to cross the sea, but is so frightened that he does not trust the ship. And so he stays where he is, and is never saved, because he will not get on board and cross over.

5 Faith and reason

Key word

Fideism: the view that certain beliefs are beyond the scope of reason and must be accepted on faith.

Fideism is the view that central tenets of religions cannot be shown to be the case by rational argument, but must be accepted on faith. Hence reason has no place. However, such a view can be challenged. C Stephen Evans (*Thinking about Faith*, 1985) points out that:

> *In a pluralistic culture it is almost impossible not to reflect critically on where one should place one's trust. (p. 20)*

Also our ability to reason can be seen as a gift from God. Therefore it would seem right to use that ability when faced with a variety of conflicting religious claims.

Key question

What is the relationship between faith and reason?

A distinction is often made between believing something by faith and believing something by reason. However, this may be false. Faith is acting on what you have good grounds to think or know is true – a leap, but not a leap in the dark, or an irrational step. Often faith involves weighing the evidence. Basil Mitchell propounded a story about the resistance movement. A partisan meets a stranger whom he believes is the secret leader of the resistance movement. Sometimes the stranger appears to be working against the movement, but he is told that this is all part of the stranger's plan. The partisan continues to believe the stranger. Likewise religious belief continues, often when there seems to be contrary evidence. The believer weighs the evidence and assesses what is the most reasonable and consistent overall view. For instance, a Christian has faith in the love of God as shown by the Cross, despite the contrary evidence of suffering in the world. He would claim that such a position of faith was not unreasonable.

Evans (*Thinking about Faith*) comments that:

Key quote

'a faith which evades critical questions is a faith that lacks confidence, which is not truly assured it has found truth.'

EVANS

> *a faith which evades critical questions is a faith that lacks confidence, which is not truly assured it has found truth. (p. 177)*

He argues that if God wants us to freely choose to love and obey Him, then God couldn't make it *irrational* to be a theist. Hence the theistic 'proofs' could be seen as one aspect by which we choose freely by means of our rational faculties.

6 Pascal's wager

Key people

Blaise Pascal (1623–62) was a French mathematician, philosopher and Christian apologist. He provided a different approach from the emphasis on certainty that was a feature of his times.

The French mathematician and philosopher Blaise Pascal presents an interesting approach to religious belief. In 1654 he had a religious experience and became a devout Christian. Afterwards, by means of his famous wager argument, he tried to persuade his friends to give up their hedonistic way of life and become pious Christians. He argued that God couldn't be known by argument and evidence.

The evidence for God is ambiguous. Equally Pascal did not see religious belief as a cold intellectual judgement (belief-that) but rather as an emotional, passionate conviction (belief-in). Hence argument alone could not produce that emotion of the heart.

As a result he developed what has become known as Pascal's wager. He argued that it was sound judgement to act as though there existed a God who grants eternal happiness to those who sincerely believe in Him. Pascal taught that those who sincerely sought God by living what he called the 'religious life' (that is, living piously, going to Mass) would come not only to give intellectual assent to the existence of God but also to experience the reality of God in a heartfelt way. He believed that personal faith was the way to eternal life.

The wager involved a choice that could not be avoided in life. We have to choose either to live as though God existed or live as though God did not exist. Pascal argued that it is unreasonable to be an atheist. For if the theists were right, they would win eternal happiness as opposed to annihilation. What the theist would be giving up would be short-term pleasures of a life of self-indulgence and gratification. The atheist would have gained a life of pleasure at the cost of eternal happiness.

However, if the atheist is right, and there is no eternal happiness, then the theist will have lost some of life's pleasures. Yet the atheist gains little more – just a few pleasures of this life. Hence good judgement requires us to risk the wager (stake) of living pious lives. It appeals more to self-interest than to the truth of God.

Needless to say, many have questioned the logic of Pascal's arguments:

- Pascal offers the choice between God existing and God not existing. However, the actual choice is between the Christian God and no God. It does not consider the option that there might well be a God but not the one that Pascal was advocating. Hence the theist could still be condemned for following the wrong God.
- Pascal makes a step of faulty logic. He argues that there are a number of religions in conflict and therefore only one is true. However, a set of contrary beliefs do not demand any of them to be true. They may all be false.
- The persuasion of the wager assumes a God who will annihilate the unbeliever. However, what if God is forgiving? It would then give the atheist not only pleasures in this life but also eternal happiness with God in the next life!
- Pascal assumes that God will condemn those who have unbelief even though he accepts that the evidence for believing is not intellectually convincing. Surely it would be morally wrong of God to condemn those who cannot believe because they do not have the evidence?

Key question

What is meant by the term Pascal's wager?

Key question

Is it better to believe in God than not to believe, even if it turns out that God does not exist?

Key question

What happens if God is not the Christian God?

Key question

What difference would it make to the argument if God is a forgiving God?

Key question

Would a moral God condemn someone who felt unable to believe?

- Would it not be morally wrong of God to reward those who only believe because of self-interest and greed?
- It is not guaranteed that living a life of faith as though one were a believer necessarily results in the faith that God requires. To act as if one believed does not guarantee that one will believe.
- If the wager is rejected, it is by no means certain that an atheist cannot become a Christian by some other means. Indeed there are countless examples of atheists becoming Christians by other means, so maybe to remain as an atheist, rather than live as though one were a believer, might be more likely to result in conversion.

Key quote

'It is not always irrational to choose an action that carries with it a slender chance of an infinite loss.'

M CURD

Pascal never included the idea of hell (eternal damnation) in his argument. However, this would not change the argument. M Curd (*Argument and Analysis: An Introduction to Philosophy*, 1992) comments that it may be logically impossible for a perfectly good God to condemn anyone to eternal damnation, since it would be unfair to have an endless punishment for finite human wickedness.

Figure 17 Pascal's wager

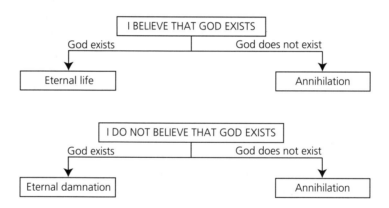

Study guide

By the end of this chapter you should know and understand the differences between belief-that and belief-in, and be able to critically assess the issues concerning the relationship between belief and evidence. Different understandings of the word 'faith' should also be understood including its relationship to reason. Finally you should be able to critically assess Pascal's wager argument.

> ## Revision checklist ✓
>
> Can you name **four** scholars linked to the topic of belief and faith and state what contribution each have made to the debate?
>
> Do you know the difference between the following?
>
> - Belief-that–belief-in
> - Faith–belief
> - Reason–evidence.
>
> Can you state **three** criticisms of Pascal's wager?
>
> Can you give responses to those criticisms?

Example of exam question

Assess the role of faith in supporting religious belief.

A good answer would include a variety of views with some critical analysis, as the question has an evaluative (AO2) trigger. Lower level answers would tend to present only one view in any depth and critical evaluation would be limited. For higher level answers it would be expected that candidates would discuss a negative view of the role of faith where beliefs were seen as without justification or even irrational. Such faith might be seen as having little value. Candidates might then contrast this with a view that saw faith taking precedence over reason (e.g. Kierkegaard). Very good answers might comment that some religious beliefs may be deemed to be beyond our reasoning and so require faith. If reason were sufficient, then there would be no room for faith.

High level answers might also discuss the importance of reason together with faith. Faith is necessary to move the believer from the merely intellectual assent, to a commitment and trust relationship with God.

The evaluative (AO2) skill will be the way candidates express these differing views and reason their case. Weaknesses of the arguments should be identified and an appropriate conclusion reached.

Further questions to consider

1 'It is possible to believe that God exists but not have religious faith.' Discuss.

2 Assess the claim that if the existence of God were proven, there could be no religious faith.

11 THE PROBLEM OF EVIL

Chapter checklist

This chapter examines the philosophical problems raised by the classic expression of the 'problem of evil'. Various theodicies are considered and their strengths and weaknesses assessed.

1 The problem stated

Key people

Epicurus (342–270BC)
was a Greek philosopher who founded Epicureanism and taught that the highest good was pleasure or freedom from pain.

Key quote

'Either God cannot abolish evil, or He will not; if He cannot then He is not all-powerful; if He will not then He is not all-good.'

AUGUSTINE

Key question

Why is evil a problem?

Key word

Classical theism: belief in a personal deity, creator of everything that exists and who is distinct from that creation.

The so-called 'problem of evil' was first formulated by Epicurus (342–270BC), and has been restated in various forms down the centuries. Augustine (354–430) in his *Confessions* expressed the dilemma as:

> *Either God cannot abolish evil, or He will not; if He cannot then He is not all-powerful; if He will not then He is not all-good.*

The assumption is that a good God would eliminate evil as far as He is able. Given that He is all-powerful, He should eliminate it all. However, evil exists. In other words God has the means (power) and the motivation (love, goodness) to eliminate evil. So why does He not do it?

When put in its simplest form it is seen as essentially a logical problem:

- God is omnipotent.
- God is all-good.
- God opposes evil.

Therefore evil does not exist in the world.

The argument seems to be valid, at least from a theistic point of view, in that believers in God would agree with the premises. However, most would admit that evil does exist. There is therefore a contradiction, and if one is to remain logical it suggests that one of the premises is wrong. However, that would deny **classical theism**. In one sense, the problem is really only a problem for the believer in God. If there is no God there is no problem.

Key questions

What is moral evil?

What is natural evil?

Key quote

'Nearly all the things which men are hanged or imprisoned for doing to one another, are Nature's everyday performances.'

JS MILL

Key questions

What is the origin of evil?

How is the problem of suffering different from the problem of evil?

It is usual for philosophers to include God's omniscience in God's omnipotence, for a God who can do anything, but does not always know what is the best way of doing it, might be said to be less than all-powerful. Also, it is usual to maintain that God cannot do the logically impossible, for example, make square circles. Neither can He do what is inconsistent with His nature. However, it must be acknowledged that philosophers still debate these points. 'God is all-good' implies that He opposes evil and will wish to remove it. Attention is often drawn not just to the presence of evil in the world, but to whether the existence of God is compatible with the amount of evil in the world.

The illustration of evil is an important aspect of clarifying what the 'problem of evil' actually is, since different types of evil raise different philosophical issues. It is usual to divide evils into:

- Moral – which arise from the responsible actions of groups and individuals who cause suffering or harm. They include such things as stealing, lying and envy, as well as the evils of some political systems.
- Natural – which arise from events which cause suffering but over which human beings have little control, for example, earthquakes and disease.
- Some make further groupings such as physical – which refers to pain itself and mental anguish – and metaphysical – which refers to imperfection and contingency as a feature of the cosmos.

At various times certain events have been used as classic illustrations of evil. At one stage it was the Lisbon earthquake of 1755, but in the present day it is the Holocaust that illustrates moral evil, and AIDS, cancer or the tsunami of 2004 that illustrate natural evil.

A further issue is the actual origin of evil. If God created or caused all things, then clearly He is the originator of evil. The fact that God is all-powerful and so all-knowing also raises problems about our free will and hence responsibility for doing evil. Also the fact that God is the originator and doer of evil implies that followers of God should copy His example.

The problem of suffering highlights a slightly different emphasis. It focuses on the *experience* of the evil. It raises different questions because of the experience. It deals with the problem on a more personal level, namely, how does the individual respond to suffering? The questions that are raised here are more of the form: Why me? Why now? Why this particular form? Why this intensity? Why this length? These seem to be questions that struggle to find purpose and explanation in what is being experienced.

Quite clearly, the rather academic and cold discussion about the philosophical problems of evil are often inappropriate for someone battling with their own personal pain and grief, and this raises questions of whom the discussion is aimed at. Possibly most discussions have been levelled at the atheist, and an attempt has been made to show that evil is not logically incompatible with the existence of God. Such attempts include Swinburne's 'free-will defence' which particularly concentrates on the problem of the *amount* of evil. In contrast, others focus on the moral issue, assuming God exists but unsure whether one can trust such a God. Such a stance is found in the character of Ivan Karamazov in Dostoyevsky's novel *The Brothers Karamazov* (1880). Likewise, John Roth's 'protest **theodicy**' is addressed to such an audience. Yet another audience are believing theists who want to understand why God allows evil. Such books as CS Lewis' *The Problem of Pain* (1940) fit this category. As I said earlier, being in anguish does make a difference to how one approaches the problem of evil and many books have been written from this perspective. *A Grief Observed* (1961) is a classic book by CS Lewis about the death of his wife.

It is important to recognise the different audiences to whom the writings on the problem of evil are addressed, since they are written for different purposes, to achieve different results. Hence in assessing an argument, it seems unfair to accuse it of saying nothing about some issues, given that it was only attempting to address another issue, and unfair therefore to conclude that what it says is worthless.

Many have argued that there is a contradiction involved in the fact of evil and the belief in an omnipotent all-loving God. However, it does not seem logically contradictory, since it is not the same as saying 'there is a God and there is no God'. It is not logically necessary that an omnipotent, all-loving God prevents evil, and a theodicy is an attempt at a solution of the problem of evil, without denying God's omnipotence or love or the reality of evil. It shows how God is justified in allowing evil. The word 'theodicy' is from the Greek *theos* meaning God, and *dike* meaning righteous. Alternatively, a defence argues why it is reasonable to believe that God has reasons to allow evil without actually demonstrating that those are the reasons. Hence, theodicy could be defined as a philosophical and/or theological exercise involving a justification of the righteousness of God. Clearly, this justification requires the theodicist to reconcile the existence of an omnipotent, omniscient and morally perfect divinity with the existence and considerable scale of evil.

I think if I were to try and state what all the theodicies share in common in their solution, it would be that evil is a necessary condition or consequence of some otherwise unachievable good, which God desires to create. This could be summarised as all being justified by some kind of greater good, for example, free will or a maturing process.

Key word

Theodicy: a justification of the righteousness of God, given the existence of evil.

Key question

Is the fact of evil and a belief in an omnipotent all-loving God a logical contradiction?

Key question

What do the theodicies have in common?

Figure 18 The problem of evil

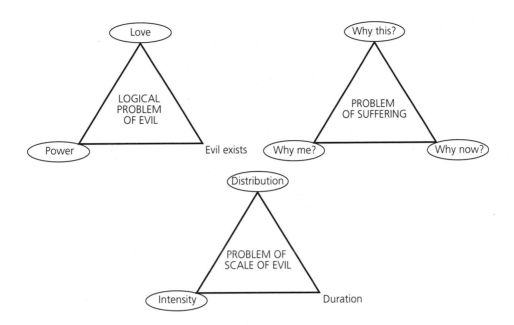

2 Some possible approaches

a) Does evil exist?

One approach to the problem of evil is to deny the problem by denying the existence of evil. Monism states that everything is of one nature; assuming that this nature is good rather than evil, it means that evil is an illusion. Monists would acknowledge that we may 'feel' that such a view of reality is false since we 'seem' to experience evil. However, our feelings are false.

In reply, Ninian Smart (*Philosophers and Religious Truth*, 1964, p. 140) commented that even if 'from the standpoint of eternity' we are mistaken in our imaginings of suffering, we will still have experienced what other people would regard as real suffering.

b) The nature of God

Another approach to the problem would be to challenge the nature of God: either His goodness or His omnipotence.

Key question

Is God all good?

Key people

Elie Wiesel (b 1928)
a Holocaust survivor and author of
Night which described experiences
in a concentration camp.

i) God is not all-good/all-loving

This suggests that God is generally unconcerned about destroying
evil and so presents a rather sadistic picture of the character of God.
Clearly this is not the God of classical theism because it requires
God to be morally imperfect.

However, recent writings, for example, John Roth (in
Encountering Evil, ed. Stephen Davis, 1981) and Elie Wiesel (*The Trial
of God*, 1979), particularly in the aftermath of the Holocaust, have
seen the development of a 'protest theodicy'. Given God's
omnipotence, events in history such as the Holocaust demonstrate
that such a wasteful God cannot be totally benevolent. In the
foreword to Wiesel's play *Trial of God*, he recounts an occasion when
he saw three rabbis put God on trial in Auschwitz, find Him guilty
and then go off to pray. It is that sort of tension that this theodicy
advocates. In a sense it is not a new response since it follows the
pattern set by Abraham, Moses and Job, all of whom contended
with God. The Psalms are full of protest to God (for example,
Psalm 90). Nevertheless, despair is not the response, but rather a
defiance of God, reminding Him of His promises and a risky hope
for the future. Such an approach has brought forth criticisms such as
whether a God depicted by this theodicy is worthy of worship.

ii) God is not omnipotent

Key question

Is God all-powerful?

This would provide a solution by recognising that God is incapable
of destroying evil. For instance, dualism argues for two co-eternal
substances locked in conflict and that the continuance of evil is
indicative of the lack of power of God. Certainly such a view can be
found in ancient mythologies of Greece and Rome and contributed
to the belief that matter (for example, the body) was evil.

A modern form of this approach is called '**process theology**'.
Amongst its proponents are AN Whitehead and David Griffin. The
problem of evil is removed by redefining the meaning of
omnipotence. It is a reaction against the classical Christian
theodicies in which God seems unaffected by our suffering, even
immune to it, and this world and its experiences are seen as
relatively unimportant. The emphasis in salvation on escaping from
this realm illustrates such views.

Key word

Process theology: emphasises
'becoming' rather than 'being'.
God is not seen as omnipotent
but is changeable and persuasive.

In contrast, process theology stresses this life and maintains that
the most real thing about a person is the series of experiences
which make up the process of their life here and now. God is seen
as one intimately involved with this world and its suffering. Indeed,
God is called a 'co-sufferer'. The different understanding of God's
omnipotence derives from process theology's view that creation was
not *ex nihilo* (out of nothing). Rather, creation was the achievement
of order out of a pre-existing chaos. This limits God's power since
these pre-existing materials are not totally subject to God's will.

Key question

What is the nature of the God of process theology?

Hence God is depicted not as a powerful, almighty despot but rather as someone who creates by persuasion and lures things into being. God is in time and both affects and is affected by the world. He even depends on His creatures to shape the course of His own experiences. Such a God cannot control finite beings, but can only set them goals which He then has to persuade them to actualise. Evil occurs when such goals are not realised. Natural evil is also explained. For instance, Griffin states, 'If cancerous cells have developed in your body, God cannot lure them to leave voluntarily' (in *Encountering Evil*, ed. Stephen Davis, 1981).

Needless to say, such a view has not passed without criticism. It is seen as a major departure from the God of classical theism. Certainly it is admitted that there is no guarantee that good will ultimately overcome evil. It is not even clear that there is life after death, and some process theologians speak in terms of existing in the memory of God.

3 The two classical theodicies

In Western history there have been two main theodicies, those of Augustine (354–430) and Irenaeus (130–202).

a) The Augustinian theodicy

It should be noted that Augustine approached the problem from different angles; his various thoughts on the issue can be found in a number of his writings including *The Confessions* and *The City of God*. It is difficult to conclude exactly what Augustine's answer was since he had strands of thought rather than a worked-out theodicy. The central theme of Augustine's thought is that the whole creation is good. It is also a realm that has great variety of forms of existence, each having its appropriate place in the hierarchy of being. As God is the author of everything in the created universe, it follows that evil is not a substance, otherwise it would mean that God created it, which Augustine rejects. Thus for Augustine, evil is a **privation**. A privation is the absence or lack of something that ought to be there. It is the malfunctioning of something that in itself is good. For instance, sickness is a real physical lack of good health. Evil cannot exist in its own right. Evil enters when some member of the universal kingdom, whether high or low in hierarchy, renounces its proper role in the divine scheme and ceases to be what it is meant to be.

God created *ex nihilo* (out of nothing) as opposed to *ex Deo* (out of God). God cannot be less than perfect but his created beings can be destroyed or deprived. God cannot be the author of this corruption, so for Augustine the answer is found in free will. It is good to be free but with that freedom comes the capability of

Key word

Privation of good: an absence or lack of good. A malfunctioning of something that in itself is good.

Key quote

'You are free to eat from any tree in the garden; but you must not eat from the tree of the knowledge of good and evil, for when you eat of it you will surely die.'

GENESIS 2:16–17

actualising evil. Augustine argues for a belief in the fall of angels and of man. God foresaw man's fall 'from the foundation of the world' and planned their redemption through Christ. In Augustine's writings it seems clear that he saw the angels that fell as predestined by God to do so. In the case of man he sees that, through Adam, all are in a state of guilt and condemnation but God brings some to repentance and salvation.

From these general ideas have stemmed a number of variations so that it is usual to refer to theodicies that use Augustine's main ideas of privation, the fall and free will as 'Augustinian-type theodicies'.

Augustine (354–430CE)

Augustine was Bishop of Hippo, in north Africa, and is regarded as the first major Christian philosopher. He was distinctive in that he thought through philosophical issues in the light of his faith and his understanding of the Bible. His various approaches on the issue of the problem of evil can be found mainly in *The City of God* and in his autobiography *The Confessions*.

b) Criticisms of Augustinian-type theodicy

Key questions

Is Genesis literal?

Is God to blame?

i)   Modern science rejects the picture of a fall of humanity from perfection. Rather it suggests an evolutionary development. A literal approach seems to contradict modern science. Hence, some have taken the book of Genesis as a symbol/myth depicting the fact that all humans do sin, by choice.

ii) If humans are finitely perfect, then even though they are free to sin, they need not do so. If they do, then they were not flawless to start with – and so God must share the responsibility of their fall. (Note that Augustine argues that some angels were predestined to fall. If this view is not accepted then how did angels fall, given that they were perfect?) Surely in a perfect world they would have no reason to sin? In response, it is argued that God could have brought about a world where creatures were free but never sin, since Jesus was free to sin and did not. Alvin Plantinga (*God, Freedom and Evil*, 1974) argues that it is logically impossible for God to create another being such that it by necessity freely performs only those actions which are good. For God to cause them to do right would be a contradiction of their freedom. Others have argued along different lines, pointing out that even if it is logically possible, not everything logically possible is actually achievable. Love cannot be programmed. The fact that heaven is pictured as containing people who will never sin suggests that perhaps God could have created such beings on Earth. However, we will have chosen to be in heaven which may entail some restrictions to our free will as a result.

iii) It is hard to clear God from responsibility for evil since He chose to create a being whom He foresaw would do evil. Many see 'love' as the key to this issue. God wishes to enter into loving relations with His creatures. But genuine love is an expression of the free commitment of both parties. Love between God and His creatures is therefore possible only if the creatures are free – that is, if they are able to reject His love as well as respond to it. Without freedom we could not share in God's goodness by freely loving Him. Nevertheless, the creation of free creatures involved the risk that persons would misuse their freedom and reject the good, and this is what happened. God could have chosen to make a world without free creatures in it. This would mean that the creatures would be robots, and therefore it would be a non-moral world. It may be physically better but it cannot be regarded as morally better, since it is non-moral.

iv) The existence of hell is not consistent with an all-loving God. Hell seems contrary to a loving/good God. As a result, some argue that all are saved whilst others suggest annihilation rather than eternal damnation and suffering.

v) Augustine's view of evil as a privation is challenged. It is not sufficient to say that it is a lack or absence. Many would argue that it is a real entity.

vi) If everything depends on God for its existence, then God must be causally involved in free human actions. Do we have free will?

c) The Irenaean theodicy

In general terms, the Augustinian theodicy is a **soul-deciding** theodicy. In contrast, the Irenaean theodicy is **soul-making**. In the writings of Irenaeus (130–202), there appears the idea that humans were not created perfect but are developing towards perfection. Irenaeus distinguished between the 'image' and the 'likeness' of God (Genesis 1:26). Adam had the form of God but not the content of God. Adam and Eve were expelled from the Garden of Eden because they were immature and needed to develop, that is, they were to grow into the likeness (content) of God. Thus they were the raw material for a further stage of God's creative work.

John Hick (*Evil and the God of Love*, 1968, p. 290), commenting on this further stage, says:

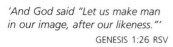

> *it is the leading of men as relatively free and autonomous persons, through their own dealings with life in the world in which God has placed them, towards that quality of personal existence that is the finite likeness of God …*

The fall of humanity is seen as a failure within this second phase (likeness), an inevitable part of the growing up and maturing. The presence of evil helps people to grow and develop. Thus the emphasis in this theodicy is *soul-making*.

Irenaeus himself never developed a full theodicy as such, but his approach represents the type put forward by Friedrich Schleiermacher (1768–1834), and in more recent times by John Hick. Hick sees the first phase, of God making man in His image, as the culmination of the evolutionary process, whereby a creature has been evolved who has the possibility of existing in conscious fellowship with God. The second phase involves an existence of making responsible choices in concrete situations. It is a necessary pilgrimage within the life of each individual. The value of this world is:

> … *to be judged, not primarily by the quantity of pleasure and pain occurring in it at any particular moment, but by its fitness for its primary purpose, the purpose of soul-making.* (Evil and the God of Love, *1968, p. 295*)

Hick goes on to argue that:

> … *in order to give people the freedom to come to God, God creates them at a distance – not a spatial but an* **epistemic distance** [*a distance from knowledge of God*]. *He causes them to come into a situation in which He is not immediately and overwhelmingly evident to them.* (p. 317, my emphasis)

In other words, the world is ambiguous and it could equally well be reasoned that there is no God as strongly as there is a God.

An essential part of this theodicy is that this process is worthwhile because of the eventual outcome. If the process is not completed in this life, then Hick argued that there is another life in another realm to which we go, until the process is complete.

The reason why God creates imperfect rather than perfect beings is twofold, according to Hick:

- Human goodness that has come about through the making of free and responsible moral choices, in situations of difficulty and temptation, is more valuable than goodness that has been created ready-made.
- If humans had been created in the direct presence of God they could have no genuine freedom. Hence the epistemic distance. It is best that free beings freely choose to love God.

The Irenaean-type theodicy also has an element of 'greater goods'. For instance, some moral goods are responses to evils and hence could not exist without them, for example, courage, compassion, forgiveness. Sometimes this is referred to as a '**second-order good**'. The moral goods are those that result from alleviating,

Key people

John Hick (b 1922)
is an English theologian and philosopher who has been influential in popularising a soul-making theodicy. He has also argued for religious pluralism. Hick has developed the Irenaeus theodicy in his book *Evil and the God of Love*.

Key word

Epistemic distance: a distance from knowledge of God. God is hidden and so this allows human beings to choose freely.

Key question

Why would God create imperfect beings?

Key word

Second-order good: a moral good that is a response to evil.

resisting and overcoming evil and involve intelligent and informed responses to evils. This could be seen as a necessary part of the soul-making process.

Irenaeus (130–202CE)

Irenaeus is thought to have been a Greek from Smyrna (modern-day Izmir in Turkey). He was raised in a Christian family and became the second Bishop of Lyon. Almost all of his writings were directed against gnosticism, which he considered a heresy. Gnosticism preached a hidden wisdom or knowledge which was only given to a select group. This knowledge was necessary for salvation or escape from this world.

One of his most influential arguments concerns the conception of human beings as created imperfect. This theory later influenced Eastern theology and was used by John Hick for his modern soul-making theodicy.

Irenaeus is referred to as an 'Early Church Father'. This is the term used of the early and influential theologians and writers in the Christian Church, particularly those of the first five centuries of Christian history. It does not generally include the New Testament authors.

d) Criticisms of Irenaean theodicy

Key questions

Is it possible to never get to heaven?

Does the end justify the means?

i) If the end result is guaranteed by God, what is the point of the pilgrimage? Indeed, if there is universal salvation, then do we have free will to refuse to mature? Some point out that we could forever refuse, while others comment that there is infinite time. This issue of the end result being realised is crucial to the theodicy. If the end result is not realised, then how can the evil experienced be justified?

ii) Does the end justify the means? The suffering experienced (for example, Auschwitz) cannot justify the ultimate joy. Indeed, in the Holocaust, people were ruined and destroyed more than made or perfected. It is hard to see how this fits God's design and human progress.

iii) Could not the greater goods be gained without such evil/suffering? For instance, cannot co-operation be learnt by teaming together to win an athletics match?

Key word

Atonement: the reconciliation of human beings with God through the sacrificial death of Christ.

iv) As a Christian theodicy, it seems to make the **atonement** superfluous and unnecessary. The response is that Jesus is an example to show us one who has the content of God. Perhaps a more Christian approach would be to see the theodicy more in terms of 'faith-making' than 'soul-making'.

v) A number of criticisms involve suggestions of better ways to achieve this process. For example, why did the natural environment have to be created through a long, slow, pain-filled evolutionary process? Why could an omnipotent God not do it in 'the twinkling of an eye'? Equally, if we go on to another life to reach maturity, then why did God not simply make our earthly spans much longer, so that we could reach the Celestial City on earth, or at least get closer? Indeed, is there any evidence for other lives? (see chapter 13).

e) The free-will defence theodicy

Key question

What is the free-will defence theodicy?

Implicit to both the Augustinian and the Irenaean theodicies is the free-will defence. It is argued that the evil that exists in the world is due to humanity's misuse of the gift of free will. God wished to create a world in which created rational agents (that is, human beings) could decide freely to love and obey God. Recently Swinburne (*The Existence of God*, 1979) has addressed the problem of the sheer quantity of evil, which many feel is unnecessarily large. He points out that a genuinely free person must be allowed to harm herself and others. God could intervene to stop her or let her learn from consequences. However, the latter is more in keeping with the exercise of moral freedom.

Key people

Richard Swinburne (b 1934) is an Oxford professor of philosophy who has devoted himself to promoting arguments for theism.

What of free choice to bring about death? Swinburne argues that death is good in that it brings an end to suffering. It would surely be immoral for God to allow humans to have unlimited power to do harm. Also actions matter more when there is a limited life. Death makes possible the ultimate sacrifice; it makes possible fortitude in the face of absolute disaster. When it comes to the Holocaust, he says 'the less God allows men to bring about large scale horrors, the less the freedom and responsibility He gives them'. In other words, we can make real choices.

Key quote

'the less God allows men to bring about large scale horrors, the less the freedom and responsibility He gives them.'

SWINBURNE

For Swinburne, natural evil is necessary so that humans have a knowledge of how to bring about evil. Rational choices can only be made in the light of knowledge of the consequences of alternative actions. He cites the example of earthquakes. A choice of building on earthquake belts, and so risking destruction of whole populations, is only available if earthquakes have already happened due to unpredicted causes (see *The Existence of God*, p. 208).

f) Pain and suffering

Hick comments in *Evil and the God of Love* (1968) that the removal of pain in a material world would require:

> *... causal regularities to be temporarily suspended ... and would approximate to a prolonged dream in which our experience arranges itself according to our own desires. (pp. 341–42)*

One can intend to harm someone only if one thinks it is possible to do so. Richard Swinburne has argued that an intention to cause harm supposes the knowledge that certain sorts of behaviour will cause harm and an appreciation of what pain, mental anguish and other harms are like. As we have seen, some argue that suffering is sometimes necessary for a higher good to be achieved, for example, courage.

Attempts at understanding pain and suffering will be dependent on which theodicy one favours. Those in the Augustinian tradition would see it as the result of the fall of man and the consequence of rebelling against God. Shouts of 'Why doesn't God do something?' receive the reply of 'God has' – in that the Cross is the ultimate solution. God has reversed the effects of evil both here and now, and ultimately. The Bible suggests that linking your life with God starts putting evil in reverse, so that in heaven pain and suffering will be totally absent.

Another Biblical idea is that God suffers with us. He is with us in our suffering. Also the omnipotent God can turn evil and suffering to good account. Alternatively, the Irenaean tradition sees it as necessary for soul development. It is through suffering that character and virtues are often developed. The Old Testament story of Job describes him as suffering as part of a test. The test is whether he will continue to love God, in spite of his sufferings. The outcome is that Job ceases to look for an explanation – it is sufficient to experience God. On an individual level this is the Christian approach to coping with pain and suffering, recognising that it is a Christian responsibility to work for the removal of evil.

g) Natural evil

JS Mill said in *Three Essays on Religion* (1874):

> *Nearly all the things which men are hanged or imprisoned for doing to one another, are Nature's everyday performances. Killing, the most criminal act, Nature does once to every being that lives!*

The Augustinian tradition would argue that our rebellion against God has affected all of creation and distorted it, so that our environment is not as God intended it (Romans 8:22). In addition, Augustine saw natural evil caused by fallen angels who by their free decisions wreak havoc.

Others note that things like volcanoes and earthquakes are in themselves neutral. Like a powerful waterfall, there is nothing inherently evil in them; rather, they become evil when people are hurt by them. Hence some have argued that if we had remained in perfect fellowship with God, then God would guide us away from these dangers, and hence we would not be hurt by them. In this case they would not be regarded as evil. An illustration of this is of a three-year-old child living near a busy road or deep river. Both are life-threatening but, close to and protected by her parents, both road and river can be a source of usefulness and life. In contrast, the Irenaean theodicy sees natural evil as the best possible agent for the purpose of soul-making. It is also part of the epistemic distance.

h) Animal suffering

Reconciling animal suffering with a good God causes many people the most difficulties. This is because it seems to have no connection with free moral actions, nor brings about a greater good. Attempts at a justification include:

- Denial that animals feel pain.
- Animals are different from humans in that we recall past and predict future, hence reflect on our suffering.
- Most animal sufferings occur when they are removed from their natural habitat. CS Lewis develops this idea in his book *The Problem of Pain* (1940).
- Pain is not useless. Although animals do not have a moral nature to develop, they are physical and pain can act as a warning system.
- The natural order has been affected by the fall of man and perverted animal life.
- In some way animals serve the soul-making process, possibly by contributing to the 'epistemic distance' by which man can exist as a free and responsible creature – free to harm God's creation.
- Natural selection aids evolution.

i) Conclusion

Are the theistic responses adequate? Certainly many people find the existence of evil a persuasive argument against the existence of God. It is an issue that affects every one of us and so moves beyond the merely academic interest.

Figure 19 Augustinian and Irenaean theodicies

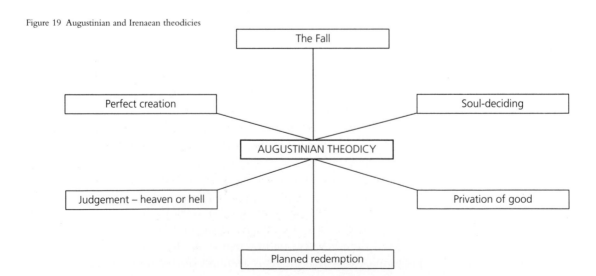

Figure 19 Augustinian and Irenaean theodicies *continued*

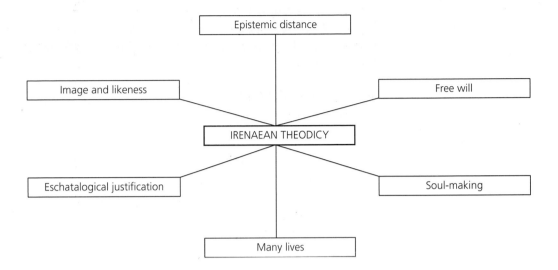

Study guide

By the end of this chapter you should know and understand why the existence of evil raises problems for classical theism. In addition to this, you should be able to explain and critically assess the main theodicies that have been proposed in attempts to resolve the problem of evil.

Revision checklist

Can you explain how each of the following words/phrases is connected to the problem of evil?

- Theodicy
- Epistemic distance
- Second-order goods
- Privation of good.

Do you know the difference between the following?

- Soul-making–soul-deciding
- Process theodicy–protest theodicy
- Natural evil–moral evil
- Theodicy–theology.

Can you list the strengths and weaknesses of each of the main theodicies discussed in the chapter?

Example of exam question

'If God were the omnipotent, wholly good, creator of all things, then evil would not exist. Evil exists. Therefore, God is not the omnipotent, wholly good, creator of all things.'

Examine this argument.

Lower level answers will tend not to make specific reference to the particular quote given. The logic of the quote needs to be explained. God has both the means and the motivation to remove evil. Higher level answers will also discuss the phrase 'evil exists'.

The AO2 would involve examining some theodicies that challenge the conclusion and assessing their strengths. Higher level candidates might well challenge the actual premises, for example, does evil exist? Process theodicy might be referred to, as it denies the omnipotence of God and therefore changes the classic form of the argument.

Lower level answers will tend to go for breadth whilst higher level ones will tend to go for depth. As a result the weaker answers will tend to result in a 'list' approach rather than understanding and evaluation being demonstrated.

Further questions to consider

1 'The problem of evil can never be satisfactorily solved.' Discuss.

2 'The Irenaean theodicy is unacceptable as an answer to the problem of evil.' Discuss.

3 Compare and contrast the approaches associated with Augustine and Irenaeaus to solving the problem of evil.

12 THE MIND AND BODY PROBLEM

Chapter checklist ✓

This chapter examines various views about the relationship between the mind and the body. A number of models are looked at and their strengths and weaknesses assessed. Finally, the issue of personal identity is considered.

1 Mind and body?

Key question

Is body different from mind? If so, how are they related?

Key word

Qualia: felt experiences such as tasting a hamburger.

Before discussing the issue of life after death (chapter 13), it is necessary briefly to consider the nature of humans. Our views about the different models relating mind and body will influence our views about personal identity and what constitutes a person. This in turn will affect the way we understand such concepts as resurrection and reincarnation.

Human beings appear to be characterised by both body (physical) and mind (consciousness) properties. Your body can be defined as the mass of matter whose weight is your weight. It has size, shape, mass and spatial and temporal position. It is composed of recognised material stuff such as carbon. It has physical properties such as height. Your height is a fact, whatever you may think about it. It is independent of a person's conception, that is, their mental processes.

An example of a mind property would be thinking about your height, or self-consciousness. This is dependent on your conception. The characteristics of mind include **qualia** and intentionality. Qualia is qualitative rather than quantitative. It concerns felt experiences such as tasting a hamburger. John Puddefoot (*God and the Mind Machine*, 1996) explained qualia as 'properties of the inside-out world that cannot be seen from-outside-looking-in'. Intentionality means 'aboutness': I don't just think, I think *about* something. In contrast, it does not seem sensible to speak about tables directing their attention on an object. They have no attention to direct!

It is because of these sorts of properties that many philosophers make a distinction between body and mind. The problem is whether mind and body are one and the same nature (monistic) or whether we do have two natures (dualistic). If they are two separate entities, then a further problem arises as to how they interrelate.

2 Dualism

Key word

Dualism: a fundamental twofold distinction, such as mind and body.

Dualism has been the prevalent view. Dualists argue that people have composite natures, namely material and non-material. The non-material element is usually called the soul, spirit or mind. It should also be stated that many argue for soul and mind being different, in that the soul represents the spiritual aspect of man, whilst the mind is more linked to the brain and related to reasoning, etc.

The Greeks saw the body as a tomb or prison of the soul. The ultimate destiny of the soul was to be released from the body. This sort of idea is inherent in the Hindu idea of reincarnation, where the aim of the soul is not to be reincarnated into another body, but to be absorbed into the oneness of God (Brahman). In contrast, the traditional Christian view is expressed in terms of a resurrection of the body. The relationship envisaged could be phrased as 'My body is my soul's proper home. My soul is my body's proper master' (Arthur Custance, *The Mysterious Matter of Mind*, 1980, p. 81). However, it should also be noted that recent Christian thinking has tended to emphasise the person as a whole (holistic) and hence has moved towards a more monistic understanding.

Key quote

'My body is my soul's proper home. My soul is my body's proper master.'

A CUSTANCE

a) Interactionism

The classic presentation of dualism is by Descartes. He argued that the body is spatial and in no sense conscious, whilst the mind is non-spatial and is conscious, having thoughts, feelings, desires, etc. As regards the interrelationship of the body and mind, Descartes favoured interactionism. This holds that states of consciousness can be causally affected by states of the body, and states of the body can be causally affected by states of consciousness. In other words, the mind and body can interact. An example would be drugs changing my perceptions and a nightmare causing me to scream out. Descartes further reasoned out that the point of interaction was in the brain. To be more precise, he sited it in the pineal gland, the one structure in the brain that is not duplicated. As to how these two natures interact, Descartes remained agnostic.

The problem posed by the idea of something non-spatial causally affecting something spatial was deemed so severe that alternative dualistic models were proposed. Parallelism held that the mind and body are like two clocks, each with its own mechanism and with no

Key people

Descartes (1596–1650) is regarded as the founder of modern philosophy. He was a dualist and argued for interactionism as the theory that related body and mind.

causal connection between them, yet always in phase, keeping the same time. One clock had face and hands but no bells to strike the hours whilst the other had bells but no face or hands. To an onlooker it would seem that there was a causal relationship between the two clocks since the bells of the one rung when the other showed the hours. However, it is because they were regulated and ran in parallel that they exhibited a harmony. Parallelism proposed a similar idea for the harmony of the mind and body. The regulator was seen to be God.

b) Epiphenomenalism

Another variation is **epiphenomenalism**. This holds that bodily events can cause mental events. However, mental events cannot cause physical events, in other words, the mind cannot control the body. Indeed, what happens is that the mind is a by-product of brain activity. Electrical impulses move between brain cells and produce 'thinking', 'imagining', etc. Thinking and so on are not the electrical impulse. The mental is 'above' (*epi*) those more fundamental processes (*phenomena*) of brain events. A popular analogy is that of a shadow to the person. The shadow cannot affect the person. The causation is one-way.

Support for dualism has come from the work of the neurosurgeon Wilder Penfield and his research on epileptic patients (*The Physical Basis of Mind*, 1950). Exposed brain tissue of conscious patients had electrodes applied to it. The result was a double consciousness. They were aware of their immediate surroundings and of vivid, re-enacted scenes from their past. Penfield concluded that 'if we liken the brain to a computer, man has a computer, not is a computer' (p. 108). Further weighty support for dualism has come from the work of Sir Karl Popper and Sir John Eccles. Although they differ as to the origin and destiny of the mind, they both argue for interactionism in their book *The Self and Its Brain* (1977).

c) Conclusions

Even if there are two natures, it could well be that both perish at death. Indeed, it would be odd that given their interaction, one should be mortal and the other immortal. Alternatively, one may argue that given two natures of very different kinds, it would be odd not to consider that one might survive death.

Clearly the relevance of dualism for life after death is that it becomes a possible concept that our soul/mind/spirit does not cease when our body decays. Rather it can have an existence of its own or can be re-clothed. Whatever it is, it suggests that something that is 'us' could continue on at death. Evidence from extra-sensory perception and near-death experiences would add support to this view. For further discussion see chapter 13.

3 Materialism

Key people

Gilbert Ryle (1900–76)
was a philosopher who is principally known for his critique of Cartesian dualism. He coined the phrase 'the ghost in the machine'.

Key word

Category mistake: the mistake committed when an object or concept that belongs in one category is treated as if it belongs in a category of a different logical type.

Key words

Philosophical behaviourism: mental events are really ways of referring to complex patterns of behaviour.

Materialism: the existence of matter only.

This view argues that so-called mental events are really physical events occurring to physical objects.

Recent years have witnessed severe criticism of dualism and a rejection of the illusive and illusory, non-material other self. One of the most famous attacks on dualism came from Gilbert Ryle in his book *The Concept of Mind* (1949). He described Descartes' model as 'the ghost in the machine'. The 'ghost' is the mind and the 'machine' is the body. He was indicating that he did not think that the mind, as a separate entity and nature, existed. Ryle rejected the idea of the mind as a different kind of thing from bodies. He believed such misunderstanding came about because of a **category mistake**. By this he meant that brain and mind belong to different logical categories which have been wrongly associated together. An illustration that Ryle used to clarify the phrase was that of a foreigner visiting Oxford or Cambridge for the first time and being shown a number of colleges, libraries, departments and offices. He then asks, 'But where is the University?' Ryle points out that this 'was mistakenly allocating the University to the same category as that to which the other institutions belong' (*The Concept of Mind*, ch. 1). He searches for the University (mind) but is presented with colleges and libraries (body). The mistake is that he searches for the University as though it were a separate entity, when in fact he had already found it.

a) Philosophical behaviourism

The alternative theory that Ryle argued for was **philosophical behaviourism**. This saw all supposed 'mental' events as really a way of referring to a complex pattern of behaviour. Ryle sees the term 'mind' functioning as a collective noun, like 'University' in the previous example, and so mind is no longer something internal but now comes to mean what we do with our bodies. We say someone is depressed because of the behaviour pattern they show, in other words, it is **materialism** because mental terminology actually means something physical (behaviour).

The obvious difficulty arises when a person in a particular mental state (for example, wishing) does *not* behave in any particular way. This is overcome by introducing the concept of a disposition to behave, where appropriate behaviour is regarded as potential and can be anticipated given certain circumstances. Thus 'wishing' can be analysed in terms of physical behaviour even though it is not translated on every occasion into actual behaviour.

Most feel that this is an inadequate approach as an answer to the mind/body problem. Although it may be possible to refer to other people's mental states by reference to behaviour, it surely fails when

THE MIND AND BODY PROBLEM 125

we refer to ourselves. When I say that 'I feel pain,' I am not referring to the way I behave. Furthermore, not all mind states can be expressed as behaviour states. For example, what of someone who pretended? There would be no difference in behaviour between the person who believed and the person who pretended to believe. Also, it does not seem to answer the problem of our own self-consciousness – something that does not show itself necessarily in any behaviour pattern.

b) The identity theory

Key word

Identity theory: the mind and the brain refer to the same object but they have different meanings.

An attempt to overcome these difficulties is the **identity theory**. Instead of trying to analyse the meanings of mentalistic terms, it argues that mental and physical events are one and the same. The names 'mind' and 'brain', whilst having different meanings, nevertheless refer to the same object. A popular example concerns the offices of the Vice-President of the United States and the President of the United States Senate. They do not have the same meaning but they do refer to the same individual. When I say 'I have a pain,' I do not mean the same thing as when I say 'I have such and such a neural process.' However, they are identical. Certainly the developments in neurosurgery that link a thought/action with a particular part of the brain have popularised this theory of the mind/body relationship.

Key people

Gottfried Leibniz (1646–1716) contributed both to philosophy and mathematics which included logic and analysis.

The major philosophical attack on this solution revolves around Leibniz's law of identity. This maintains that if things are identical then they must share identical properties. Thus opponents draw attention to such things as a wicked thought (mind), noting that a brain state (body) cannot be said to be wicked, and therefore Leibniz's law is not obeyed. In response, the supporters argue that Leibniz's law does not apply to intention states. A wicked thought is an intention state since it refers to a particular way of representing, thinking or conceiving that thing.

c) Functionalism

Key word

Functionalism: expressing the mind and body relationship as descriptions of their causal roles.

The most recent approach to the mind/body problem is called **functionalism**. Analogies with computers are made where the software descriptions centre on their function. So in the same way, mental states can be defined in terms of their function (job description) or causal role. For example, the function or job description of pain is as a tissue damage detector. Pain inputs include tissue damage and trauma. Pain outputs include groans and escape behaviour. Thus all mental states can be seen as having a causal role. The concept of the mental state is therefore of an internal state caused by certain sensory inputs and causes certain behavioural outputs. It is this sort of model that makes some researchers of artificial intelligence argue that computers can think.

d) Conclusions

So what are the implications of materialism?

Key question

Are we morally responsible?

- *Moral responsibility* – it is difficult to see how free will is compatible with the theory that all brain events are physically determined. However, Donald MacKay (*The Clockwork Image*, 1974, p. 79) argues that it is possible. He speaks in terms of the 'logically indeterminate'. By this he means that even if it were possible to know all factors that caused brain events and be able to predict future action, it would still mean that the actual action could be different. The reason is that if that prediction were made known to the person, they would not be under constraint to follow it. The eventual outcome would thus result from a decision and therefore could be deemed to involve 'responsibility'. In reply it is said that in fact even this decision is ultimately physically determined and is merely an illusion of freedom.

Key questions

What is the nature of the universe?

Is there life after death?

- *Nature of the universe* – do we live in a causally enclosed physical universe or is there a metaphysical realm? For discussion of the paranormal, see page 137.
- *Life after death* – dualism seems to favour survival more than does materialism, when continuity after death is considered. Those who favour materialism have often argued for a replica theory approach where the whole person is recreated after death. For discussion of this, see page 132. The interesting philosophical question that arises from such a view is whether 'the recreated person can be accurately described as being the "same" person they were before they died'.

Figure 20 Materialism and dualism

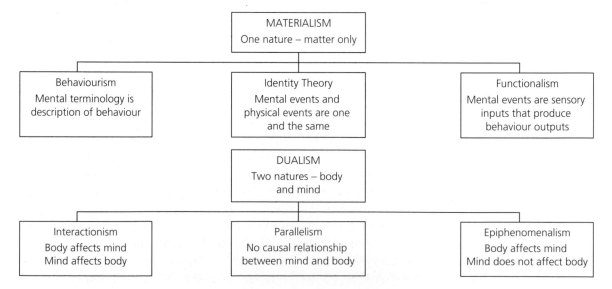

4 Personal identity

Key questions

What are the criteria for deciding what constitutes a person?

What are the criteria for someone to be regarded as the same person?

Key people

John Locke (1632–1704)
was a British philosopher who was an empiricist. He developed a theory of mind and argued that continuity of consciousness was a key aspect of 'self'.

This is important for the philosophical approach to the study of life after death. Two issues in particular emerge:

- What criteria are there for deciding exactly what constitutes a person? Can what makes a person be isolated and identified?
- What are the criteria that are necessary for somebody to be regarded as the same person? For instance, if someone ceases to be, then reappears, what has to be true for the reappearance to be regarded as the same person as the one who ceased?

Philosophers have tried to tease out these criteria by inventing various scenarios that attempt to isolate exactly what constitutes a 'person'. By varying the scenarios it is possible to examine whether the characteristic that is isolated is the essential ingredient that makes a person a person. Possibly the classic illustration originates from John Locke. He told the story of the cobbler and the prince, where the two characters appear to wake up with each other's body. The 'cobbler' woke up in the palace and wanted to explain that he had not broken in but could not explain how he got there. However, he had the appearance of the prince. Meanwhile, the 'prince' woke up in bed next to the cobbler's wife and accused her of kidnap and demanded to be taken back to the palace. He had the body of the cobbler. The problem is how to decide which is the cobbler and which is the prince. Which ingredient counts – the body or the memory? To which do you attach the person? Is it a case of bodily transfer or memory transfer? Certainly the body lends itself to being a suitable means of verifying who a person is. The boundary of our skin clearly separates us from the rest of the external world. Our body also has continuity through space and time. However, the above illustration casts doubt on our certainty in identifying people in this way. Many feel that the body is not the essence of a person.

Another famous illustration is taken from Franz Kafka's story *Metamorphosis* (1916), in which the main character Gregor is transformed into a beetle. Does Gregor still exist? Certainly many regard this illustration as suggesting that the 'person' is the mind. Is my body 'me' or 'mine'? Is a brain transplant the only case where we would prefer to be donor rather than recipient?

Perhaps the reaction of self-interest is a clue to our view of personal identity. For instance, would you be happy stepping into a transporter machine that destroyed every cell but identically copied them at arrival? And what if the machine went wrong and produced lots of duplicates of you! Science fiction has been a great source for such illustrations. John Hosper's book *An Introduction to Philosophical Analysis* (fourth edition, 1997) has excellent examples on this in chapter 6. See also *How to Live Forever* by S Clark (1995).

For many the concept of a person is more than just a living human being. What of people who suffer from Alzheimer's disease? Often partners and relatives claim that they are 'not the same person'. Yet is Descartes' description of a person as 'a thinking thing' really sufficient? Is a robot a thinking thing? If so, is a robot a person? As has been mentioned, the conclusions about personal identity will be very much influenced by views about models of mind and body. Clearly it is also a vital issue when assessing views about life after death, and whether a 'person' survives death.

These are the main suggestions of criteria for personal identity:

Key question

What is the criteria for personal identity?

- *Body* – there is continuity, though it is accepted that it changes with time. For example, if John is the same person today as he was yesterday, there must be continuity between the two. John's body gives him that 'continuedness'. However, resurrection and reincarnation do pose problems for this view.
- *Memory* – certainly this is what is unique about each individual and it also enables us to relate to our yesterdays, though what happens if I forget or have the wrong memory? Many philosophers argue that you need physical identity to verify memory, otherwise how can it be known that it is the same person?
- *Brain* – research on the brain by, for example, Penfield has suggested that each hemisphere has a separate consciousness with its own sensations, perceptions, learning experiences, memories, etc. If the two parts were transplanted into separate skulls, would both be the same person? For further discussions about this, see Jonathan Glover's book *The Philosophy and Psychology of Personal Identity* (1988).
- *Personality* – a problem with this suggestion is that people have multiple personalities, so which one is the 'real' person? Recent research suggests independent centres of control within a person and so counts against any idea of unity.
- *Personhood* – perhaps the 'I' is flexible and consists of a number of things, such as rational thought, consciousness, self-consciousness and emotions.
- *Soul* – this is a similar idea to personhood with the addition of freedom and moral responsibility, relationship to God and determination towards supreme value. The soul finds deepest fulfilment in seeking a growing union with the supreme reality of God. Its proper purpose and true nature lie beyond the physical universe. A popular analogy is of a butterfly emerging from a chrysalis – it may be able to disentangle itself from properties of the brain and exist in a new mode.

- *Non-owner* – this is a radical approach that suggests that the word 'I' does not refer to anything apart from a stream of experiences that 'I' is supposed to own. As Hume said, 'I can never catch myself at any time without a perception, and never can observe anything but the perception.'

It should be noted that these criteria are not necessarily mutually exclusive.

Figure 21 Possible criteria for personal identity

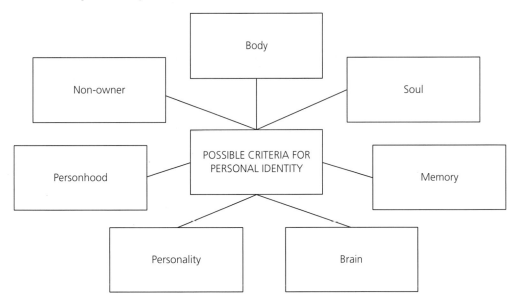

Study guide

By the end of this chapter you should know and understand the main theories that materialists and dualists have proposed as solutions to the mind and body problem. You should also know the strengths and weaknesses of these theories and be able to critically evaluate them.

Revision checklist ✓

Can you name **five** different mind/body theories and the philosophers associated with each of them?

Can you name **one** strength and **one** weakness for each of those theories?

Can you explain how each of the following words/phrases is connected to the mind/body problem?

- Qualia
- Dualism
- Category mistake
- Personhood.

Can you explain the difference between the following?

- Mind–body
- Materialism–dualism
- Epiphenomenalism–identity theory
- Functionalism–behaviourism
- Personality–personhood.

Example of exam question

1a) What is meant by the mind/body problem?

b) Assess the solution to this problem by reference to interactionism.

Lower level answers for AO1 will tend to just define what is meant by 'mind' and what is meant by 'body'. Higher level answers will give some illustration and focus on the actual problem concerning their relationship.

The part b) question requires knowledge and understanding of interactionism and the success or otherwise of this approach as a solution to the problem. Lower level candidates will tend to give an account of what interactionism is, but will not relate it to how it solves the problem. Any evaluation will be in lists of strengths and weaknesses of theory.

A higher level answer will focus the material on the slant of the question (that is, does interactionism solve the problem?). The AO2 will be a reasoned argument assessing the extent to which this theory addresses the problems identified in part a).

Further questions to consider

1 a) Select and discuss the characteristic features of the relationship between mind and body.

b) Discuss the influence of these views on arguments for life after death.

2 'The identity theory resolves the mind/body problem.' To what extent do you agree with this view?

1 The philosophical problems of life after death

a) Is it meaningful?

Linguistic philosophy challenges whether it is even meaningful to talk of life after death. Antony Flew suggested that the concept of life after death was contradictory. In his essay 'Can a man witness his own funeral?' Flew likened the phrase 'surviving death' to 'dead survivors'. To classify the crew of a torpedoed ship into 'dead' and 'survivors' is both exhaustive and exclusive (that is, it covers all possibilities and no one can be in both groups). Likewise with 'surviving death' – it is self-contradictory and therefore meaningless.

Schlick claimed that it was not only conceivable but also imaginable that you could witness your own funeral. Flew challenged this by arguing that if 'you' are viewing your funeral, then what you are witnessing is not 'you' but your body (an empty shell). In a sense this is playing language games and does not deny the meaningfulness of life after death. A dualist (see page 122) view would answer both of Flew's criticisms.

In his essay in *New Essays in Philosophical Theology* (1955), Flew argued that words such as 'you', 'her', 'I' and 'Peter' are person words referring to physical organisms and have meaning only in this context. They indicate actual objects which you can point at, touch, see, hear and talk to. Thus it is non-meaningful to apply such words to either an immaterial or a spiritual body newly created by God.

Key question ?

Can you witness your own funeral?

Key people

Moritz Schlick (1882–1936) was a member of the Vienna Circle (see page 147).

Antony Flew (b 1923) is a British philosopher. Known for several decades as a prominent atheist, Flew first publicly expressed deist views in 2004.

Key quote

'[There is] no reason why the meaning of words should be indissolubly tied to the contexts in which they were originally learnt.'

AJ AYER

However, AJ Ayer (*The Central Questions of Philosophy*, 1973) commented that there is 'no reason why the meaning of words should be indissolubly tied to the contexts in which they were originally learnt'.

Paul Badham (*Immortality or Extinction?*, 1982) questions whether the personal pronoun 'I' is a person word in quite the same sense as Flew's other examples. He argues:

> There is a real difference between our subjective experience of our own selfhood and our objective experience of the individuality of others. (p. 17)

Science fiction stories involving body transfer illustrate the concept of 'I' remaining 'I' though clothed with a new and different body. Reported out-of-body experiences also display the concept of selfhood being applied to something other than the body. See section on evidence for life after death (p. 137).

AJ Ayer commented in *The Central Questions of Philosophy* that:

> If there could conceivably be **disembodied** spirits, the fact that it would not be correct to call them persons would not perhaps be of very great importance.

Key word

Disembodied existence: an existence without a body.

Confusion in language does not automatically mean that the concept being expressed has no reality.

b) Continuity

Key question

Does anything continue through death?

Advocates of materialism (see p. 124) face a major difficulty since there is nothing that could continue through death. If nothing continues, then in what sense can one say that it is the 'same' person after death? The only solution would be for the body to be recreated. MacKay (*The Clockwork Image*, 1974) draws an analogy with a chalk message written on a blackboard and then erased. Just as the message can be rewritten using chalk or some other material, or even spoken, so God could recreate us after death (pp. 78–79). The criticism is that nothing survives of the original entity, so in what sense can it be considered the same? It would be more accurate to refer to it as a replica.

i) John Hick's 'replica' theory

Key word

'Replica' theory: the theory that an identical recreation of a person constitutes them being regarded as the same person.

Indeed, the **'replica' theory** is one that John Hick argues for, following on from his theodicy of the 'vale of soul-making' (see section on the Irenaean theodicy, p. 113). Hick acknowledges that there is a problem about continuity, but through three examples he argues that it is meaningful to call it the same person if someone dies and appears in a new world with the same memories, etc. He uses the word 'replica' in inverted commas because he uses it in a particular sense – namely that it is not logically possible for the

Key question

Is someone who is a replica a different person?

Key people

John Hick (b 1922)
is an English theologian and
philosopher. He has argued for
religious pluralism. His soul-
making theodicy implies the need
for life after death, so our souls
can continue to progress.

Key question

Is a replica the same as the
original?

Key word

Dualism: a fundamental twofold
distinction, such as mind and body.

original and the 'replica' to exist simultaneously or for there to be
more than one 'replica' of the same original.

He cites three examples in his book *Death and Eternal Life*
(1976). In the first instance:

> *Someone suddenly ceases to exist at a certain place in this world and the
> next instant comes into existence at another place. However the person
> has not moved from A to B by making a path through the intervening
> space, but has disappeared at A and reappeared at B.*

Hick uses the illustration of London and New York:

> *The person who reappears is exactly similar, as to both bodily and men-
> tal characteristics, as to the one who disappeared. There is continuity of
> memory, complete similarity of bodily features such as fingerprints, stom-
> ach contents and also beliefs and habits. The person would be conscious
> of being the same person though would not understand how they now
> come to be in a different place.*

Hick argues that it is reasonable to call this person the same person
as the one who disappeared.

In the second instance, the person in London dies and a 'replica'
of him appears in New York. Again Hick argues that it would be
reasonable to regard the replica as the same person who died – odd
though it would be!

Hick's final case involves the person dying and reappearing in a
different world. Hick likens this to waking up from sleep. The
person then would regard themselves as the same person as the one
who had died.

Hence by these progressive examples, Hick argues for the idea
that a living person ceases to exist at a certain location, and a being
exactly similar to him in all respects subsequently comes into
existence at another location – namely in the next world. In this
instance Hick argues that it is valid to say it is the *same* person. For
Hick, a person is an indissoluble psycho-physical unity and therefore
the body is a necessity.

In response, philosophers such as Terence Penelhum have
challenged such a conclusion, arguing that there can only be an
automatic and unquestionable identification when there is bodily
continuity. As soon as this is lost, then it is debatable whether it is
correct to call the two people the same person. This would raise the
further problem of the appropriateness of divine judgement on such
a being.

ii) Dualism

Dualism fares better since it allows for mental continuity. However,
it involves isolating the 'ghost in the machine'. By definition, it is
not physical and therefore elusive. Popper saw the self-conscious

mind having a personality 'something like an ethos of a moral character' (*The Self and Its Brain*, 1977). R Zaehner has suggested that Hindus in meditation experience not God but their naked spirit (*Concordant Discord*, 1970). However, most see the memory as the key to continuity. Terence Penelhum (*Survival and Disembodied Existence*, 1970) expresses it formally as:

> *the person A at time T2 is the same person B at some earlier time T1 if and only if, among the experiences that person A has at T2, there are memories of experiences that person B had at T1. (p. 77)*

Key question

Are we more than just the sum total of our memories?

The problem with such a view is that most people would argue that they were more than just the sum total of their memories (see earlier section on personal identity, p. 126, for fuller discussion of the 'I').

In contrast, **reincarnation** involves the idea of the transmigration of the soul (in the sense of the conscious character and memory-bearing self) from body to body, in other words, the 'I' who is now conscious has lived before and will live again in other bodies. It involves a different body and no guarantee or need to remember past lives.

Bosch's Ascent to the Empyean

Key word

Reincarnation: the transmigration of the soul from body to body.

The problem that arises is in deciding in what sense it can be said that we keep our identity and have continuity. Many would respond by saying that it is irrelevant since what is important is the continuing development of the soul/spirit. However, without memory or bodily continuity, in what sense are we able to say that the reincarnated person is the same person as the one who lived 500 years previously?

Another problem that arises is exactly who the person is who has been reincarnated. Supposing that this is the third reincarnation. Which person of the three are you?

c) Identification

Key question

Will other people recognise us after death?

Another philosophical problem involves the awareness after death of who we are and to what extent others will recognise us. Linguistic philosophy argues that the only possibility of identifying a person is to indicate some bodily criteria. However, at death the body decomposes and ceases to be. It is true that bodily criteria are necessary for identification in the conditions of the world in which we now live. Nevertheless, that does not prove that they are therefore necessary when these earthly conditions are absent. Indeed, it is difficult to understand what would be meant by 'the same body' after death. During our lifetime we all change physically. Indeed, our very cells change. Some have suggested that in the resurrection world we shall have bodies which are the outward reflection of our inner nature but reflect it in ways quite different from that in which our present bodies reflect our personality. If so, presumably people would recognise us. Perhaps God would ensure that others recognised us.

People such as Terence Penelhum have pointed out that even physical identity is no guarantee of identity. He quotes the fictional story of the cobbler and the prince (see page 127). This raises the problem of what criteria we use to identify and is a particular problem for reincarnation theories.

Of course, it is a questionable assumption that identification is relevant after death.

d) What kind of life?

Here the difficulty lies in applying our normal concepts of personal life to a post-mortem being. As regards resurrection – although the modern tendency in Christian theology is to regard man as a psycho-physical unity, there may be a strong case to retain the dualist view with the mind/soul surviving death and being clothed in a new body. An alternative would be to argue that the individual continues to exist in the mind of God between death and resurrection.

The New Testament gives an indication of the form of the resurrected body, if we regard Jesus' resurrection as a prototype. It could be touched and bore resemblance to the earthly body (Luke 24:39). Yet at times it was not recognisable (Luke 24:13–32). Also it was not limited in the way that our bodies are, for instance, it could pass through matter (John 20:19) and disappear (Luke 24:51).

Some do not regard Jesus' resurrected body as the final spiritual body. Support for this is found in John 20:17 which suggests that the ascended body was different. Also Paul likens the relationship of the earthly, physical body to the spiritual body using the analogy of the seed to the full-grown plant (1 Corinthians 15).

However, if Christians are in a physical, resurrected state and physical environment, will they have to queue to see Jesus? Where will this physical existence be? And what will they be doing all the time? Similar questions are raised about hell, though there is a modern tendency to reject this concept and favour annihilation.

Clearly the disembodied survival raises more problems than the doctrine of a resurrected body, since all the physical elements that make up our lives are inconceivable without a body. Disembodied persons cannot walk or talk, though psychical research and out-of-body experiences may suggest otherwise (see section on evidence for life after death, p. 137). The cases which tend to arouse the most

Key question

What kind of life will it be in our post-mortem existence?

Key quotes

'... when the disciples were together, with the doors locked for fear of the Jews, Jesus came and stood among them ...'
JOHN 20:19

'Jesus said to her, "Do not hold me, for I have not yet ascended to the Father."'
JOHN 20:17

Key question

What sort of body would we have after death?

interest among psychical researchers are not the cases where spirits are alleged to move physical objects, but cases where they are alleged to communicate by speaking through the mouths of mediums. This suggests the possibility of spirits occupying the bodies of people for short periods.

Out-of-body experiences suggest physical abilities through mental states, but this happens in a physical realm where items have form. If nothing had form (only mental states), then the difficulty about the type of life may remain.

The most famous work in this area is by HH Price (*Survival and the Idea of 'Another World'*, 1953). He argued that perhaps the next world is not in space. Instead it could consist of internal processes only – a dream world, where each person would have their own private dreams. However, it could still contain real communication and interaction with other minds, for example, via **ESP** (extra-sensory perception). The mental images acquired during the embodied existence would presumably be the source of the dreams. From the person's point of view the world would appear 'real' and 'solid' and existence may well appear to be bodily. However, the sequence and arrangement of events may be discontinuous as they are in our dream world, since the post-mortem world would be governed by laws of psychology rather than of physics.

If the next world is fashioned by our desires, then it may not be pleasant. They might reveal our true characters, including those that have been repressed. Ultimately this could be repugnant to our better nature. Hence we could develop our desires into something better and move to higher moral worlds.

John Hick (*Death and Eternal Life*, 1976) argues that if the mental worlds are created by our desires, then it may be that many people will exist in isolation with no communication with others. In these cases he questions the quality of life and asks whether this is really 'living'. However, he solves the problem of the non-identical private worlds by suggesting the creation of a common shared world from everyone's mental images. All are pooled to produce a common environment, each contributing but not exclusively. Hick likens it to a superimposition of a great number of individual photos. However, this would be forever changing as new sets of desires were added with each new 'dead' person 'arriving'! The alternative would be a number of separate worlds, as Price suggests. This could lead to highbrow and lowbrow worlds and worlds with endless philosophical seminars. Yes, we could be talking *real* heaven or hell!

Perhaps the major problem is that such views about the afterlife are not seen as consistent with traditional Christian teaching.

Key people

Henry H Price (1899–1984) was a British philosopher who wrote on perception and parapsychology.

Key word

ESP: extra-sensory perception.

Key questions

What would life created by our desires be like?

What problems are raised by the idea of mental worlds created by our desires?

Heaven is a world that is given to us and for us. It is not something that we create ourselves. However, Hick does argue that the mental image world could fit with his theodicy of soul-making, though not the final state.

2 The evidence for life after death

On a gravestone in York, there is an inscription that reads:

Remember friend when passing by,
As you are now so once was I.
As I am now you will be.
Prepare for death and follow me.

Underneath someone has scrawled:

To follow you I'm not content,
Until I know which way you went.

a) Psychic evidence

The belief in life after death has come under attack from various quarters. Modern advances in the sciences have seemingly supported a monistic and natural world view rather than a dualistic and supernatural one. Equally, the growth of secularisation has led to a rejection of traditional religious beliefs. One area of evidence to support life after death comes from psychical research.

In 1882, the Society of Psychical Research was founded to investigate evidence for the paranormal (known also as parapsychology). This area is relevant to life after death as it supports dualism and suggests that the power of the mind is such that thoughts and actions can be transmitted between the living and the dead. Evidence from such research can be divided into five main categories.

i) Telepathy

Telepathy is the name given to a thought in our mind being 'picked up' by another without normal communication. In 1934, Dr Rhine at Duke University in America published the results of tests based on the use of **Zener cards** (*Extrasensory Perception*, 1934). Zener cards are a pack of 25 cards showing five each of several simple symbols: plus sign, star, circle, square and three wavy lines. These were shuffled and turned over one at a time by a 'sender' while a 'receiver' tried to guess the cards as they were turned. Similar results have been obtained by other researchers, though various criticisms are raised about the actual experiments and the interpretation of the data. John Hick (*Philosophy of Religion*, 1983) concluded that 'it is difficult to deny that some positive factor and not merely "chance" is operating' (p. 129). This factor is referred to as ESP (extra-sensory perception).

Key words

Telepathy: the communicating of mind with mind.

Zener cards: a pack of 25 cards showing five each of several simple symbols: plus sign, star, circle, square and three wavy lines.

Key people

Dr Rhine (1896–1980) investigated telepathy and established the parapsychology department at Duke University. The term 'extra-sensory perception' (ESP) was coined by him.

ii) Psychokinesis

Dr Rhine also made a study of **psychokinesis** (PK). This is the ability to move objects using the power of the mind. Helmut Schmidt, Rhine's successor at Duke University, produced a machine for testing this ability. The random appearance of an electron caused one of a series of bulbs arranged in a circle to light at random. The task of the PK subject is by the power of the mind to light the bulbs in order. Experiments seem to indicate that some people have succeeded. One of the most spectacular PK demonstrations said to have taken place involved a Russian housewife, Nelya Mikhailova, who separated the yolk of an egg from its white. A more recent example is Uri Geller who has convinced some that he can bend metal spoons, whilst others regard him as a very skilled stage magician.

iii) Spiritualism

Both telepathy and PK are seen to support **spiritualism** where, through a medium, contact is said to be made with the afterlife, for, if it were possible to pick up messages from other living people's minds, then it may be possible to pick up messages from the spirits of the dead. Also the spirits of the dead may be able to affect physical objects in our world by means of something akin to PK. The name '**poltergeist**' (literally noisy spirit) refers to the occurrence of such a phenomenon. Needless to say this whole area has been rife with fraud. Some classic cases are recorded by Arthur C Clarke (*World of Strange Powers*, 1985). Investigation into spiritualism was one of the main reasons for the formation of the Society for Psychical Research.

In considering the possibility that someone who has died may communicate with the living in this way, we are presuming the continued existence of that individual as a persisting consciousness and will, a still-living personal being. We are supposing her to be carrying on a career of some kind in the next world, and in the midst of this occasionally to take time to visit her equivalent of a medium. We are assuming therefore that the dead have a real life of their own, continuing to develop through time as persons. However, such a picture is lacking, according to John Hick (*Death and Eternal Life*, 1976). The spirits do not seem to speak out of the context of a continuing life; they seem to lack a credible environment of their own, a community of which they are a part, real next-world tasks, interests and purposes. They seem to be very much what they were in this world. And for this reason Hick argues that they are not spirits from the next world but more akin to residues of memory and traits that persist after death and that some people are able to 'pick up', that is, residues from this life, not the next world.

Other possible alternative explanations of spiritualism include:

- *Telepathy* – the information given by the medium is gained by ESP from the living, not the dead.
- *Evil spirit* – this is the traditional Christian view, arguing that the spirit contacted is a masquerading evil spirit whose aim is to confuse and mislead people about the afterlife and God.
- *Psychokinesis* – poltergeists are really the unconscious PK abilities of a living person in close proximity to the manifestation.

Key question

Are there such things as 'ghosts'?

Equally, many explanations for 'ghosts' have been offered. Some suggest that when a violent event occurs (for example, murder) an unknown force is generated to form a 'psychic image' at the place where the event happened. The image continues to exist by absorbing energy, such as heat, and can be seen by people sensitive to the psychic force. Alternatively, ghosts are explained as delayed telepathy. If the mind has an independence of time, then it could pick up vivid pictures from the minds of people from the past.

Key word

Near-death experience: an out-of-the-body experience occurring at the time of actual or threatened imminent death.

iv) Near-death experiences

Out-of-body experiences (OBEs) are cited as evidence of the spiritual element (soul) existing in its own mode without the body. Often this experience seems to occur to people who have been near to death, or even been declared dead but then resuscitated, and is referred to as near-death experience (NDE).

In 1995, Peter Fenwick detailed a study of over 300 NDEs in his book *The Truth in the Light*. He lists twelve features, admitting that the events described don't always occur in the same order, and that few people experience every event:

Key people

Peter Fenwick (b 1935) is a neuropsychiatrist and a leading clinical authority on near-death experiences.

- feelings of peace
- out of body
- into the tunnel
- approaching the light
- the being of light
- the barrier
- another country
- meeting relatives
- the life review
- the point of decision
- the return
- the aftermath.

Cases cited by Paul Badham (*Immortality or Extinction?*, 1982, chapter 5) show the accuracy of descriptions by patients as though viewing from above and looking down on their own body.

A recent study was published on 15 December 2001 in the international medical journal, *The Lancet*. It was a thirteen-year study

Key question

Is there any evidence for NDEs?

Key people

Raymond Moody (b 1944)
is a parapsychologist who coined the term 'near-death experience' (NDE). His writings pioneered, and created popular interest in, the phenomenon of NDE.

Key question

Are there natural explanations that explain NDEs?

of NDEs observed in ten different Dutch hospitals and looked at 344 patients who were successfully resuscitated after suffering cardiac arrest. Rather than using data from people reporting past near-death experiences, researchers talked to patients within a week of suffering clinical death and being resuscitated. (Clinical death was defined as a period of unconsciousness caused by insufficient blood supply to the brain.) About eighteen per cent of the patients in the study reported being able to recall some portion of what happened when they were clinically dead; and eight to twelve per cent reported going through 'near-death' experiences, such as seeing lights at the end of tunnels, or being able to speak to dead relatives or friends. In 2003, Dr Bruce Greyson published an article in *General Hospital Psychiatry* in which he describes a three-year study of 1595 patients hospitalised in a cardiac care unit. Ten per cent of patients with cardiac arrest and one per cent of patients with other heart problems had NDEs.

One of the earliest popular books on this subject was *Life after Life* by Raymond Moody (1975), in which he coined the phrase 'near-death experience'. It was this book that really brought this topic to the public forefront. Although accounts bear similarities across cultures, there are also some clear cultural differences. In particular, Carol Zaleski (*Otherworld Journeys*, 1988) researched cases of medieval NDEs. She found that the subjects were obsessed with the pain of hell and included vivid accounts of being eaten by dragons and attacked by serpents and toads. Also there were accounts of 'test bridges' where the person faced an ordeal to be allowed to cross them. These seem clearly to reflect cultural influence and, whatever else they may be, they are not simply literal accounts of the afterlife. Many argue that NDE does not show life after death since the subjects are not dead, only near to death. Explanations suggested to explain this phenomenon include:

- Change of blood pressure can evoke a floating sensation.
- Oxygen reduction to the brain can cause hallucinations.
- Psychological response – a defence mechanism to disassociate our selfhood from our dying body.
- The effect of seemingly looking from above is really the creation of our world from memory.
- Accuracy of accounts may be due to ESP or knowledge of hospital life.
- The dark tunnel effect is the dim memory of transit through the birth canal.

To counter such naturalistic explanations, various accounts are cited of children recognising 'dead' relatives in the afterlife, of whom they had no previous knowledge. Peter Fenwick of the Institute of Psychiatry has commented that pilots do not recount NDEs when they suffer loss of oxygen in simulation practice. Equally, when the brain is disrupted you do not get clear vision or coherency. For a discussion of the evidence for NDEs, see chapter 7 of the Religious Experience book in the Access series.

v) 'Remembered' lives

Key question

Is there evidence for reincarnation?

This can be a spontaneous remembering, though the most dramatic evidence has come from hypnotic regression. Arnall Bloxham has produced some well-authenticated examples of subjects recalling details of past lives. Under hypnosis, subjects have taken on a different personality, speaking with different voices and sometimes even in a different language. Also some of the historical details, when checked, have been found to be accurate and not the sorts of details that the subject would be expected to know.

Ian Stevenson has investigated numerous cases suggestive of reincarnation and for a good critical account of his studies see chapter 3 in *The After Death Experience* by Ian Wilson (1987).

Again, various explanations have been proposed:

Key word

Cryptomnesia: the memory of the subconscious.

- **Cryptomnesia** – this is the memory of the sub-conscious. Details of a historical period could have been absorbed from films and books. The mind can weave a fantasy around them.
- Genetic inheritance of the information.
- Telepathic sensitivity to the 'psychic husks' of some deceased person and identification with them.

However, as stated earlier, many would regard a mere persistence of some isolated cluster of memories as a denial of what is meant by survival after death.

b) Jesus' resurrection

Christianity expresses belief in an afterlife and claims that evidence can be found in the New Testament in the account of the resurrection of Jesus. Alternative explanations for the resurrection accounts include:

- New Testament accounts are symbolic and mythological rather than literal.
- The reports are late and one-sided and events were inaccurately remembered or passed down.
- The Disciples had hallucinations.
- It was not Jesus who was crucified.
- Jesus did not die on the Cross but was in a coma and later recovered.

Counter-arguments of orthodox Christian scholarship are that:

- Writings of the New Testament can be dated within the lifetime of witnesses. For example, 1 Corinthians was written within 25 years of the death of Jesus.

- Although written from within the Christian Church, they are written with apparent sincerity.
- The writers seriously claim that the events are historical and produce arguments for their historicity.

At the very least they claim that there is a historical case for the resurrection to be answered.

Using the structure of the diagram below, list in the empty boxes the arguments against the evidence.

Figure 22 Evidence for life after death

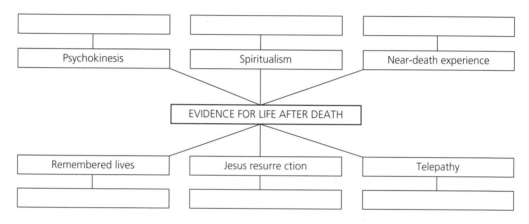

To those who already believe in the existence of a God of love, there are very strong grounds for believing that His intention is not our extinction. Keith Ward also argues that a Christian is committed to belief in immortality because of the existence of a God of love:

The whole life of faith is one of trusting that the love which we fitfully apprehend in this life will be clearly seen hereafter.

Study guide

By the end of this chapter you should know and understand the philosophical problems raised by the concept of life after death. You should also be able to discuss and evaluate the evidence for life after death, including near–death experiences.

Revision checklist ✓

Can you state **five** areas of evidence for life after death?

Can you state **four** philosophical problems of the concept of life after death?

Do you know the difference between the following?

- Dualism–monism
- Replica–reincarnation
- Resurrection–reincarnation
- Telepathy–psychokinesis
- NDE–cryptomnesia.

Can you give **two** arguments against five areas of evidence for life after death?

Example of exam question

1a) What philosophical problems are raised by the concept of 'life after death'?

b) Discuss how far such problems are capable of being solved.

Lower level answers for part a) will list one or more of the problems, but will not clearly identify the actual nature of the problem. Higher level candidates will deal with several of the problems in depth, illustrating the nature of the problem.

In part b), the lower level answers will list responses to the problems. There will be little if any reasoning or weighing up evidenced. In contrast the higher level answers will show a clear process of reasoning and assessing the strengths and weaknesses of possible solutions. They will also draw an appropriate conclusion.

Further questions to consider

1 Assess the claim that near-death experiences can never be authenticated.

2 'There is no reason to suppose that I will survive my death.' Discuss.

1 God talk

Key words

Cognitive statements: statements that are true or false in the ways that literal statements are true or false.

Non-cognitive statements: statements that are not open to truth or falsity.

Key question

What is meant by 'religious language'?

One of the strongest attacks on the arguments for the existence of God in recent times has come from linguistic philosophy. The assumption in the theistic proofs is that God is an external, independent objective being. This is to regard statements about God as **cognitive**. Cognitive statements are statements that are true or false in the ways that literal statements are true or false. However, other philosophers see religious statements as more **non-cognitive** (that is, not open to truth or falsity at all). In this other sense, coming to see that there is a God involves seeing a new meaning in one's life, and being given a new understanding. There is no new fact to discover, but rather seeing what is already here in a completely new way.

Certainly, religious talk poses difficulties. Someone may say that 'God is love'. However, it might not be clear what this actually means. What does 'God' mean? And 'love' is meaningful when used to refer to human activities – but can it be applied to God? Would it mean the same?

Another example that I have used is 'God is timeless' (*Religious Language*, 1994). As I commented:

The difficulty with this statement is that it is not possible to explain the word 'timeless'. Everything we experience happens in time and it

Key words

Correspondence theory of truth: claims that a statement is true if it corresponds to something in the real world.

Coherence theory of truth: claims that a statement is true if it coheres with other statements.

Realists: those who believe that a statement is true if it corresponds to an actual state of affairs.

is difficult to understand something that is not in time. The heart of the problem seems to be that religious terms attempt to refer to things beyond anyone's experience. They describe the 'infinite', the 'mysterious' and other metaphysical ideas that are not dealt with by our everyday language and it is thus difficult to see whether religious terms have meaning.

What lies behind these two different approaches, cognitive and non-cognitive, is a different understanding of 'truth'. The cognitive approach assumes a '**correspondence theory of truth**' as opposed to a '**coherence theory of truth**', and is followed by philosophers known as **realists**, since for them what makes a statement true or false is whether it corresponds to the state of affairs that it attempts to depict. As Peter Vardy says in *The Puzzle of God* (1990):

> *Realists maintain that reality is separate from our language and that our language stretches out to a reality that is external to us and tries to express it accurately. (p. 16)*

In contrast are the **anti-realists**, who assume a 'coherence theory of truth'. For them a statement is true if it fits in (coheres) with other true statements. Truth is relative to the community who are making the statements. So, in a sense, they *make* religious truths rather than *discover* them.

Key word

Anti-realists: those who believe a statement is true if it fits in (coheres) with other true statements. Reality is separate from language.

To understand these varying approaches and how they came about it is necessary to review how religious language has been understood in the past.

Another way of expressing the debate about realism and anti-realism with regards to religious language is to highlight two key issues. One concerns 'universals', that is, nouns like 'person' and 'goodness'. The issue is whether they are rooted:

- in some reality in things, or
- in something beyond things, or
- in human constructions.

The other key issue concerns how to interpret religious texts:

- literally, or
- allegorically, or
- symbolically.

Traditionally, there have been three main approaches to these issues, and all three were reflected in the medieval period.

a) Equivocal language about God

Key word

Equivocal: the same word is used with a different meaning or is ambiguous.

Equivocal means that the same word is used with a totally different meaning or in a vague or ambiguous way. For instance, the word 'post' can have at least two very different meanings. If language about God is equivocal then it becomes difficult to know

Key words

Via negativa: literally, the way of negation – understanding God by saying what He is not.

Scepticism: the view that we can know very little, perhaps nothing at all.

what is being stated about God. This approach led to the *via negativa* (negative way). The *via negativa* argues that it is impossible to speak of God by means of positive attributes. Instead, one emphasises what God is not, drawing attention to His otherness and unknowability. If religious language is equivocal, then by denying all descriptions of God you get insight and experience of God rather than unbelief and **scepticism**. In this approach language is functional and evocative, rather than cognitive and descriptive. However, this approach has been criticised on the grounds that theists do seem to want to make positive assertions. The listing of things God is not seems insufficiently limiting to lead to any clear attribute.

b) Univocal language about God

Whilst some figurative language may be in the Bible, it is clear that meaningful revelation has been given. Therefore religious language must be **univocal**, that is, the words used about God must have the same meaning or be as clear as the words that are used about the universe. However, some argue that the implication would then be that God is part of the universe, since the language has the same meaning.

Key word

Univocal: the same word is used with exactly the same meaning.

c) Analogical language about God

Analogy is the compromise between the other two positions. God is *not* a being like other beings *but* we can reason about Him. Aquinas argued that all such words about God are non-literal but are analogical. They elucidate the relationship between a term used of one thing and that term when used of another. Analogical language is not an instrument for mapping out the divine attributes but is a means by which we may be compared to God (father/good/loving), in order in some way to describe God's nature, when His existence is already presupposed.

Key word

Analogy: a comparison that attempts to show how two or more things are similar.

Hence, according to Aquinas, language about God is neither equivocal or univocal. For instance, God is not 'good' in exactly the same sense as people may be, nor is He 'good' in a completely unrelated way. It is argued that for the analogy to be valid there must be points of correspondence between language and its object. Colin Brown, in *Philosophy and the Christian Faith* (1968), suggests that God has revealed Himself in action, thought and word. Therefore, because of religious experience, such analogical language is appropriate and meaningful.

Key quote

'Divine truth has to be refracted and expressed in terms of human words and finite images.'

BROWN

> *Divine truth has to be refracted and expressed in terms of human words and finite images. (p. 32)*

Analogies can be subdivided into two types.

i) Analogy of attribution

This analogy contains the concept of derivation. There is a causal relationship, for example, human wisdom is a reflection of God's wisdom. Hick goes further and discriminates between 'downwards' and 'upwards' analogy. In the former case he draws on the example of a dog's 'faithfulness' to its master, saying that true faithfulness is known directly in ourselves, whereas the dim and imperfect faithfulness of dogs is known only by analogy. In the 'upwards' analogy (from people to God), it is our directly known love, wisdom, and so on which are 'the shadows and remote approximations' to the perfect qualities of God. These are known to us only by analogy. Hence, to say that God is loving is meaningful even if it is not clear what exactly it means. It is meaningful because love is a human attribute and there is a causal connection between humans and God. God is the cause of everything so God is love because God is the cause of love.

Since God is infinite, terms that are capable of infinite expression are more applicable than terms that are not. Thus 'God is loving' is more appropriate than 'God is a rock'. The latter example Aquinas calls a 'metaphor'. Surprisingly, in the twentieth century this view has been reversed and the emphasis is now on metaphors (see page 155).

ii) Analogy of proportionality

This analogy states that the attributes of God are in the same way proportional to His nature as the attributes of humans are proportional to their nature. Cabbages have life, Peter Cole has life, God has life. There is a proportionate relationship. In the case of God, the proportion is extended.

One criticism that has been raised about this approach is that proportion is only meaningful when both terms are known. But we neither know God nor the proportionate life. Therefore the analogy is seen as pointless. For a good critique of analogies, see chapter 2 in *The Philosophy of Religious Language* by Dan Stiver (1996).

2 Empiricism and the Vienna Circle

> **Key thought**
>
> Analogies between God and human beings seem to be justified because there is a casual relationship. God created human beings in his image.

> **Key question**
>
> Are analogies meaningful?

> **Key word**
>
> Empiricism: the view that knowledge is based on experience through the senses.

Twentieth-century English philosophy has been dominated by language analysis. As has been noted, both metaphysical and theological language faces the difficulty of speaking intelligibly of that which is ultimate, transcendent or perfect. The movement in the twentieth century based around logical positivism centred on the univocal approach to language. Logical positivists decided that such language, when applied to God, was not just false but meaningless! Logical positivists were so named because:

they recognised only the positive sciences (as against systems of meta-physical speculation) as valid sources of human knowledge, and in this process attended to the logical structure of scientific (that is, acceptable) statements. (G Vesey and P Foulkes, Collins Dictionary of Philosophy, *1990)*

In the 1920s and 1930s, many philosophers dedicated a lot of discussion to the 'criteria of meaning' issue. (The question may be put as 'what is the meaning of "meaning"?') They were trying to develop rules for meaningful discourse. One group of philosophers and scientists, based in Vienna, has become known as the Vienna Circle and included philosophers/scientists such as Schlick and Carnap. Accepting that knowledge is based on experience, they felt that this could also be applied to language. A criterion of meaning could be established. The Vienna Circle felt that experience is the key to determining whether a sentence is meaningful or not. They took the view that cognitive language expresses an empirical state of affairs. Determining which words can be judged either 'meaningful' or 'meaningless' is referred to as applying *criteria of meaning*.

a) The verification principle

The **logical positivists** formulated the **verification principle**, which they argued was a logical principle about the meaning of words. For a statement to be meaningful it had to be verifiable by the sense experiences (sight, touch, taste, smell, hearing). This eliminated metaphysical statements. It was not an issue about whether the statements were true or false, but rather that they were without meaning. A major influence on this group was the work of Wittgenstein (though he himself was not a member). His book *Tractatus Logico-Philosophicus* (1921) argued for a picture theory of language. This stressed that language had to be about something other than language. Meaningful language involved words being defined by the real world of objects. The meaning of a proposition lay in knowing what is pictured. To understand a proposition means to know what is the case if it is true. Unfortunately his work was misunderstood, since he believed that the mystical was important and could only be spoken about in equivocal language. He even read poetry to the Vienna Circle!

Key people

Moritz Schlick (1882–1936) was a professor in the philosophy of inductive sciences at the University of Vienna and a member of the Vienna Circle.

Rudolf Carnap (1891–1970) was also a member of the Vienna Circle. Although from a science background he later became Professor of Philosophy at the University of Chicago.

Key words

Logical positivists: a movement which developed from the Vienna Circle. They sought to find the ultimate test for meaningful statements – the verification principle.

Verification principle: the theory that sentences are only meaningful if they can be verified by the senses.

Key thought

THE INFLUENCES ON LOGICAL POSITIVISM

The logical positivist movement (which developed from the Vienna Circle) sought to find the ultimate test for meaningful statements. Its thinking was influenced by three things:

i) **Empiricism** David Hume believed that all our ideas are based on sensations (experiences); for example, we have an idea of 'trees' because we have experienced (come across) many of them. In other words, any idea we have, however complex, can be reduced to some experience that our senses have provided. Hume calls this knowledge 'matters of fact'.

Consider all the aliens we try to create in films – you can see how they all trace back to something in the real world that we have experienced. Hume's view is usually known as 'empiricism'. The logical positivists felt that experience is the key to determining whether a sentence is meaningful or not.

ii) **Science** Science was seen as a discipline that seemed to have truth. Science could assert facts and know things. Science got answers – it worked. It gave success. The key feature of science was the idea of testing things – trying to verify them by experiment. So the logical positivists thought that verification was the key in the testing for meaningfulness. Statements had to be open to verification. For a statement to be meaningful, one had to know what sense experience one would have to have, in order for it to be known to be true. Indeed this is what science did!

iii) **Philosophy and the work of Wittgenstein** Wittgenstein published a book called *Tractatus Logico-Philosophicus* in which he presented the picture-theory of language. The meaning of a proposition lay in knowing what is pictured. Words ultimately derive from our sense experiences. All words ultimately go back to an object/experience in the real world.

All these influences came together and the Vienna group (later formed into the logical positivist movement) offered the world the ultimate test for meaningful statements – the verification principle.

Key people

Alfred Ayer (1910–89)
was a British philosopher who championed logical positivism in his book *Language, Truth and Logic*, where he argued for the weak form of the verification principle.

However, this strong form of the verification principle excluded various statements that could not be absolutely verified but that many considered meaningful. For example, historical statements such as 'Julius Caesar landed at Deal in 55BC' or general laws of science such as 'All metals expand when heated' could not be absolutely verified. After all, it is not possible to observe (and therefore verify) every piece of metal every time it is heated and therefore we cannot state that all metal expands when it is heated.

It was considerations such as these that led many philosophers to shy away from such a strict application of the verification principle (although some members of the Vienna Circle, for example Schlick, argued that such things as scientific laws were meaningless: they were nonsense but 'useful nonsense'). One philosopher who attempted to reinterpret the verification principle was AJ Ayer. Although Ayer was not actually a member of the Vienna Circle, his book, *Language, Truth and Logic* (1936), is probably the most famous description of logical positivism.

Ayer argued for a weak form of the verification principle. He rejected conclusive verifiability and instead argued that, for meaningfulness, it was sufficient just to be able to know what sense experience would make the statement probable. However, even this is not possible for religious statements since 'the notion of a person whose essential attributes are non-empirical is not an intelligible notion at all' (*Language, Truth and Logic*, p. 154). He felt that, through the misuse of language, people assumed that because a word existed there must be some corresponding reality.

b) Criticisms of the verification principle

Are religious statements therefore to be considered meaningless? The verification principle should give no reason to believe this; indeed it is probably one of the most discredited theories of the twentieth century.

The verification principle cannot itself be verified. There is no sense experience that could count in its favour: the theory itself is not verifiable. Thus if we accepted the theory, we would have to argue that the theory itself is meaningless. In reply, the logical positivists said that the verification principle was not a true statement but merely a recommendation for the use of words. However, if that were so, many felt that it was a recommendation that one could ignore! It rejected statements that people felt were meaningful and therefore was not a good definition of 'meaningful'.

- Keith Ward (*Holding Fast to God*, 1982) stated that the verification principle excluded nothing, since all experiences are allowable because of the criterion of 'verifiable in principle'. He argues that the existence of God can be verified in principle since 'If I were God I would be able to check the truth of my own existence' (p. 18).
- John Hick felt that the criteria demanded by the logical positivists could be met by **eschatological verification**. He cites the illustration of two men walking down the same road. One believed that this road led to the Celestial City. The other believed that the road went nowhere. Both interpret signs along the route in different ways. However, verification is possible since there either is or is not a Celestial City. Clearly Hick was thinking of theological statements about the Second Coming and the existence of heaven. The difficulty with this approach is that there can be no disproof, for if there is no Celestial City, no life after death, no God, then there will be no one to know the falsity of the belief.
- Hick wrote about eschatological verification in response to the University debate that centred around falsification (see page 152). He was showing that there are limitations to the falsification principle, since the Celestial City could be verified eschatologically but not falsified.

Key question

Are religious statements meaningful?

Key people

Keith Ward (b 1938) is Professor of Divinity at Gresham College, London. He has written extensively on the relationship between science and religion.

John Hick (b 1922) is a noted contributor to the philosophy of religion, especially on the topics of the problem of evil and religious pluralism.

Key word

Eschatological verification: the view that some religious ideas are verifiable after death (or at the end of time).

- Theological statements are also acceptable by the verification principle since 'Jesus was raised from the dead' is a historical statement, which is therefore acceptable.
- AJ Ayer later admitted (*The Central Questions of Philosophy*, 1973) the inadequacy of the criteria for verification in that it allowed all statements to be classed as meaningful. For a fuller discussion on this, read Brian Davies, *An Introduction to the Philosophy of Religion* (1993), pp. 5–9.

It should be noted that logical positivists made a distinction between a statement that was meaningful and a statement that was true (or false). The criterion of meaning was concerned to distinguish statements that were meaningful. The issue of whether the statements were true or false was a different area of discussion.

c) The falsification principle

In the 1950s Antony Flew looked at the problem from a different perspective. He proposed that a statement was meaningless if no sense experience could ever count against it (that is, if nothing could ever happen that would change a person's belief in it being true, it could never be shown to be false and therefore was meaningless). This was known as the **falsification principle**.

Flew was prompted in this approach by the writings of a philosopher of science, Sir Karl Popper, who suggested it was not 'verifiability' with which science tested hypotheses, but 'falsifiability'. Hence Flew argued that if you knew what observation to make which would show the statement to be false, then the statement would be synthetic and meaningful. Some people regard his falsification principle as a new criterion of meaningfulness, whilst others see it as a variation of the verification criterion.

Flew illustrated this by a parable about the challenge to belief, previously used by John Wisdom. In it he clearly presupposes the falsification criterion. He tells of two explorers who discover a clearing that resembles a humanly made garden yet in other ways resembles a natural phenomenon. One explorer is convinced that there is a gardener; the other disagrees. They set about to test the hypothesis that there is a gardener, using fences, bloodhounds, and so on. No evidence of a gardener turns up. However, at every stage the believer qualifies the hypothesis: the gardener comes at night; he is invisible; he cannot be detected by any of the senses. Finally the non-believer asks: 'Just how does what you call an invisible, intangible, eternally elusive gardener differ from an imaginary gardener or even from no gardener at all?' (from 'Theology and Falsification', in *New Essays in Philosophical Theology*, 1955, pp. 96–99). Flew's claim is that this is what often happens to religious claims: 'Death by a thousand qualifications.' It is similar to

Key thoughts

There is a difference between the terms 'true' and 'meaningful'. 'Meaningful' is about whether it makes sense. 'True' is about whether it actually is the case.

'Meaningful' is concerned with whether a statement makes sense, whereas 'meaning' explains what the statement says.

Key people

Antony Flew (b 1923)
is a British philosopher who contributed to the falsification principle debate. In recent years he has moved from an atheist to a deist belief.

Key word

Falsification principle: the theory that sentences are only meaningful if some evidence can count against them.

Key people

Sir Karl Popper (1902–94)
argued that a theory should be considered scientific if and only if it is falsifiable.

Key quote

'*Death by a thousand qualifications.*'

FLEW

the response in the face of evil that says 'God's ways are mysterious.' For the non-believer there seems no difference between a God that loves, a God that does not love and no God at all!

Flew was showing that a statement can only be regarded as meaningful if some state or event can be specified, such that if it occurred it would falsify the statement. In other words, to assert something is to deny something else. Hence if nothing is ruled out, nothing is being asserted. If a statement is compatible with everything else, then it is not asserting anything. It is not saying anything unique. He felt that religious believers kept qualifying their claims to avoid falsification, which ultimately produced 'death by a thousand qualifications'.

d) Criticisms of the falsification principle

Flew seemed to be suggesting that religious assertions had no empirical consequences (since they asserted nothing), hence his view brought forth a number of responses. These were published in the journal *University* and are referred to as the 'University debate'. Strangely enough, although the debate was about univocal language, they used parables to illustrate their points.

i) Hare and 'bliks'

Hare thought Flew was right about the problem of falsification and agreed that religious language may be non-cognitive, but held that religious statements were still meaningful and important. He regarded religious beliefs as **bliks**, which was his term for unfalsifiable convictions but none the less important for the result they have on our conduct. He illustrated this by the parable about the lunatic who thought all dons were trying to murder him (see page 95).

ii) Mitchell

Mitchell agrees that statements about God are assertions but disagrees with Flew and claims that religious statements can be falsified in principle, though not in practice. He illustrates his view with the story of the resistance leader (see page 102). This parable shows that the religious believer displays an attitude of trust and that religious statements are not neutral hypotheses. It is not that things do not count against the faithfulness of the resistance leader; rather they may not decisively overturn the evidence in favour. Relating this to religious belief – evil counts against God's love – the trust is not without a sense of tension and conflict. However, if the believer has good reason to trust God's love, then evil may not be sufficient reason to overthrow that trust. Thus you can empirically falsify it, but it is difficult to say how much contrary evidence it requires to reach that point.

iii) Richard Swinburne

Key people

Richard Swinburne (b 1934) is an Oxford professor of philosophy who has strongly argued for theism.

Both Hare and Mitchell were accepting that falsification to some extent could be used as a criterion for determining meaningfulness. However, there do seem to be problems with the falsification principle. Richard Swinburne (*The Coherence of Theism*, 1977) claimed that statements can have meaning yet they cannot be falsified. He uses the illustration of toys that come to life at night only when they cannot be detected. There is no means by which the claim about toys can be falsified. However, the statement conveys meaning and hence goes against the claims of the falsification principle. Likewise, John Hick used the story of the Celestial City (see page 150) to show that some things could only be verified and not falsified, yet were still meaningful.

Like the verification principle, the falsification principle fails its own test. For the principle to count as a meaningful assertion there must be things that would count against its truth. However, it is not clear what would count as evidence against it!

Figure 23 Tests for meaningfulness

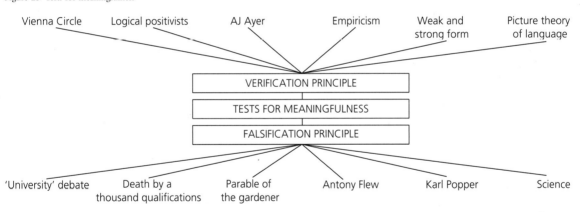

3 Symbolic language

It is now generally agreed that the ideas of 'verification' and 'falsification' are rather narrow and do not provide a criterion for establishing meaning. Many philosophers and theologians have used the idea when discussing religious language that something can represent something else. In other words, they think that it is possible to say something meaningful about God even though what they are saying may not be literal.

Key word

Symbol: something that represents something else and evokes participation.

Key people

Paul Tillich (1885–1965)
was a theologian who argued that we must go beyond the concept of God as personal agent and see faith as a state of ultimate concern.

John Robinson (1919–83)
was Bishop of Woolwich and a New Testament scholar. He argued to replace the notion of a God 'out there' with the idea of God as the depth of our being and existence.

Don Cupitt (b 1934)
is a Fellow of Emmanual College, Cambridge. A populariser of the view that the church should rid itself of all supernatural beliefs and redefine its vocabulary.

a) Symbols

This approach sees religious language as symbolic. The term **symbol** often has with it the implication of superficiality, but this is to misunderstand. A **symbol** is something that has deep communicative power and evokes participation in the intended meaning (as opposed to 'sign' which impacts on the intellect only). For instance, the Cross or the Union Jack flag are both symbols that can arouse great passion and feeling. Perhaps the best known and most radical supporter of the view that religious language is symbolic was Paul Tillich (1885–1965). He argued that 'God talk' is symbolic and cannot therefore be translated into literal assertions.

> *Symbolic language alone is able to express the ultimate because it transcends the capacity of any finite reality to express it directly. (Dynamics of Faith, 1958)*

Tillich preferred to speak of 'Being' rather than the words and deeds of a God who exists over and above the world and breaks into it. In his book *Systematic Theology* (1951), God is defined as 'that which concerns us ultimately', or 'the ground of our being'. Hence God is not a Being (who may or may not exist) but Being itself. In fact, it is just as much atheistic to say God exists as to deny it. God can be described as personal but He is not a person; if He was He would be finite. It is only the person, who in complete seriousness can say that life is shallow, who is an atheist.

This approach to the doctrine of God is still quite popular. John Robinson, then Bishop of Woolwich, in his book *Honest to God* (1963), was the most influential populariser of his views. More recently, Don Cupitt (*Taking Leave of God*, 1980) has written an attack on the traditional Christian doctrine of God and uses concepts similar to those of Tillich.

This approach by Cupitt argues that religious language should no longer be seen as being about the transcendent or the metaphysical as really it is about things that we all experience. The problems of religious language therefore disappear, as religious language is no longer seen to be about things that are beyond experience. Indeed, what religion is all about, according to some, is not some external being but our own psychology and feelings. This approach has become known as *reductionism*. For DZ Phillips (*Death and Immortality*, 1971), the phrase 'eternal life' has nothing to do with living forever; rather, it is concerned with our own psychology and the quality of life that we should be experiencing now.

Needless to say, such views have brought strong reactions. For instance, Keith Ward wrote the book *Holding Fast to God* (1982) as a direct reply to Cupitt's *Taking Leave of God*.

b) Metaphors

Key word

Metaphor: a word or phrase is applied to an object that it does not literally denote, in order to convey a resemblance.

Key quote

'The Trinity can be seen as "mother, lover and friend".'

MCFAGUE

Key word

Myth: a symbolic story that tries to explain a fundamental issue about the purpose of existence.

Likewise, a **metaphor** creates participation whereby its truth is experienced. Interestingly, the role of metaphor has taken central stage in the late twentieth century. Mark Johnson (*Philosophical Perspectives on Metaphors*, 1981) said, 'We are in the midst of a metaphormania.' Two recent contributors to this debate are Janet Soskice and Sallie McFague. In particular, Soskice (*Metaphor and Religious Language*, 1985) defends the realist claim that such language reveals something about God rather than referring to the believer's attitude or stance towards God or life. Her argument involves comparing metaphors and models in religion to their use in science (for example, 'the brain is a computer').

McFague (*Models of God in Religious Language*, 1982) sees not only religious language but also theology itself as metaphorical (that is, theology is organised by root metaphors). She also favours new metaphors since the old ones of Father, Son and Kingdom are patriarchal. She suggests that the Trinity can be seen as 'mother, lover and friend'.

It is difficult to decide whether a metaphor can successfully represent that which is beyond our experience. There seems to be no way to judge whether a metaphor is adequate. Neither is there any way to determine whether a metaphor gives the wrong insights about the ultimate (in other words, is it appropriate?).

c) Myths

The **myth** is the most complex type of symbolic language since it incorporates symbols, metaphors and models. To many people, to speak of myths is to say that something is untrue. However, a modern understanding sees myths as giving insights into human existence. The problem has been that we have applied our scientific ideas to the myths and judged the originators as naive and simple. Instead we needed to decipher them and understand that the language is symbolic. They are often associated with rites-of-passage events and so seek to provide a framework within which the whole of life can be understood. Time and space are seen as symbolic, so that those myths about origins are to be interpreted as being about all the happenings that take place in a person's time. These myths should also be seen in the context of coming from communities that held a religious outlook on the world and so interpreted life accordingly.

Probably the best-known scholar dealing with myths is Bultmann. He gave the New Testament an existentialist interpretation and many felt that he reduced it to a secular philosophy. The view that the New Testament contains many myths has most recently been expressed by David Jenkins, former Bishop of Durham.

d) Models

A twentieth-century development of the traditional idea of analogy can be seen in the work of Ian Ramsey (*Religious Language*, 1957). He saw religious language functioning as stories or **models**, qualified in various ways such that they bring about a disclosure which in turn leads to a religious kind of response – a commitment of a total kind. A model is a representation of something which assists us to understand the original. In terms of religious language a model is a 'situation with which we are all familiar, and which can be used for reaching another situation with which we are not so familiar' (p. 61).

Models are usually accompanied by 'qualifiers'. These point to the way in which the model is to be developed. For instance, consider the phrase 'infinitely good'. 'Good' is the model and 'infinite' is the qualifier. The model begins a series in our understanding of 'good'. The qualifier 'infinite' is a directive stimulating us to go on … and on … and on … until it dawns on us that when we talk of God we are not talking of something which is comparatively superior. Rather it is that which evokes adoration, wonder, worship, commitment.

In this way, Ramsey argues that the use of the word 'infinite' does not result in the language ending in an 'empirical void'. Theological phrases are not seen as labels to objective facts but the means to evoke a disclosure of that which lies beyond what is immediately observed.

e) Language/games

These ideas about language being functional and 'creating participation' rather than 'illustrating information' are based, in part, on the work of the philosopher Ludwig Wittgenstein (1889–1951). Early on in his philosophical career Wittgenstein put forward a 'picture theory of meaning'. On this view the primary function of words is to name objects and the meaning of a word is the object it stands for. Hence being wrong about meaning is being wrong about the correlates between words and things.

However, later on he re-examined the question of meaning and came to a different conclusion. He argued that it is unrealistic to suppose that all words are ultimately based on pictures and pointed out that language is used in a variety of different ways. His ideas can be found in his *Philosophical Investigations* (published in 1953, two years after his death).

Wittgenstein centred on the way that language works and the uses to which it is put. He saw that the problems of religious language were caused by the misunderstanding of language. He was not so concerned with the truth and falsity of language but with the way it was used and the functions it performed. He coined the phrase 'Don't ask for the meaning, ask for the use.'

Key word

Model: something that represents something else and helps us to understand the original.

Key quote

'The qualifier "infinite" is a directive stimulating us to go on … and on … and on … until it dawns on us that when we talk of God we are not talking of something which is comparatively superior. Rather it is that which evokes adoration, wonder, worship, commitment.'

RAMSEY

Key quote

'Don't ask for the meaning, ask for the use.'

WITTGENSTEIN

Ludwig Wittgenstein (1889–1951)

Wittgenstein was born in Vienna into a wealthy family. He studied engineering and developed an interest in mathematics and logic. After a short time at Cambridge, he joined the Austrian Army at the start of the First World War. During that wartime period he wrote *Tractatus Logico-Philosophicus* which explored the relationship between language, thought and reality. It argued for a picture-theory of language. His work was taken up by the Vienna Circle.

Later Wittgenstein changed his views and argued that language is similar to a game in that it is used differently depending on the context in which it is employed. He regarded religious belief as a way of living, an attitude to life.

Key word

Language-games: a term used by Wittgenstein to refer to any particular context in which language is used.

Key quote

'Philosophical problems arise when language goes on holiday.'
WITTGENSTEIN

Wittgenstein likened language to a game that we play. This is because at the heart of Wittgenstein's concept of '**language-games**' is the idea that words only have meaning because of their context and therefore we have to be careful to know which 'game' we are playing. For example, the word 'castling' (a move in chess) has no meaning if we are playing netball. Wittgenstein then applied this idea to philosophy and concluded that philosophical problems about language are created by not understanding that words can be used in different language-games. Hence his statement that 'philosophical problems arise when language goes on holiday'. Wittgenstein gave the example of the problems associated with the word 'soul' and argued that these problems are caused by trying to see the soul as some sort of physical object. The problems, according to Wittgenstein, would be dissolved if it was realised that the 'physical object' game simply does not apply to the soul.

The term 'language-game' is meant to highlight the fact that the speaking of a language is part of an activity. Meaning emerges in the context of human activity, not from dependence on correspondence between word and object. Wittgenstein argued that we do not so much discover the rules of how to use a word but rather we agree upon it. Hence meaning is convention! A meaning mistake is about not applying the word in the right way. The public, shared language-game is what counts as the right way. These rules Wittgenstein called 'grammar'. To say that God has big feet is not to play according to the rules because convention says that this is inappropriate to God.

The phrase/concept of 'language-games' is seen as particularly appropriate. In an article on 'Language games' in *Dialogue* Issue 7 (1996), Felicity McCutcheon drew some parallels between games and language:

- There is no unique object that can be said to be the meaning of the word 'game'. Likewise there is no one meaning of a particular word.

- There are many different games (for example, chess, netball, etc.) each of which has its own rules. Learning to play means learning the rules. Likewise with language: it involves learning what you can and cannot say.
- Games involve participation. Likewise the speaking of a language is part of an activity. Participation involves being understood (that is, playing to the rules).
- Games are not reality. Likewise meaningfulness of discourse is determined by language users and not by reality.
- Making a wrong move is equivalent to applying words in the wrong way.
- You can't do that = You can't say that.

Key quote

'Meaningfulness of discourse is determined by language users and not by reality.'

MCCUTCHEON

This understanding of religious language has led to the view that each language-game is immune from charges of incoherence and irrationality, since it has its own internal criteria of coherence and intelligibility. The danger of such a view is that each area of life develops its own unique criteria of meaning and truth. For example, Felicity McCutcheon (*Dialogue* 7) uses the illustration of the question 'Was Jesus God?' According to neo-Wittgensteinians it cannot be given a yes/no answer; rather it depends on which game you are in when you ask the question. (A Jew and a Christian might give different but equally valid answers.)

In addition, the **neo-Wittgensteinian** account of religious language has made the controversial claim that it cannot be understood as reality-depicting. It should be noted that Wittgenstein never made this judgement, only his followers (for example, DZ Phillips). However, many feel that religious statements do entail a truth that is not entirely dependent on the context. Indeed, many religious claims are claims that are believed to be true for everyone, for example, the claim in Christianity that Jesus died in order to bring salvation.

Key word

Neo-Wittgensteinian: a new or modern form of Wittgenstein's philosophy.

f) Conclusions

Not surprisingly, there has yet to appear a theory of religious language that has won general acceptance. Given that religious faith seeks to provide an understanding of reality that incorporates all the component parts of our experiences, it is to be expected that religious language turns out to be complex. Linguistic analysis has served the purpose of drawing attention to this fact, but has often fallen into the error of reductionism, as well as denying any cognitive sense. Instead, perhaps it should make us aware that many of the theories may reveal different insights into the structure of a complex whole.

Figure 24 Wittgenstein's views on language

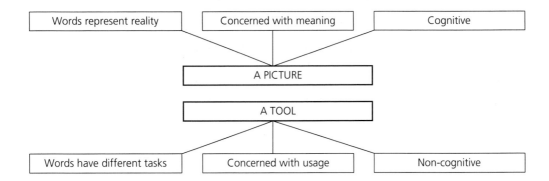

Words represent reality	Concerned with meaning	Cognitive

A PICTURE

A TOOL

Words have different tasks	Concerned with usage	Non-cognitive

Study guide

By the end of this chapter you should know and understand the problems raised by talk about God. In particular you should be able to debate the strengths and weaknesses of the verification and falsification principles. You should also know and understand the more functional approach to religious language such as language-games, and be able to evaluate these approaches.

Revision checklist

Can you list **five** scholars connected with religious language and identify their connection to the topic?

Can you explain how each of the following words/phrases is connected to religious language?

- Empiricism
- Vienna Circle
- Model
- Language-game
- University debate
- Myth.

Do you know the difference between the following?

- Verification–falsification
- Symbol–metaphor
- Myth–model
- Univocal–equivocal
- Analogy–allegory
- Attribution–proportionality.

Can you give **two** weaknesses of each of the following?

- The verification principle
- The falsification principle
- Language-games view of language
- View of religious language as symbolic.

Example of exam question

'All talk about God is both without meaning and without purpose?' Discuss.

This question involves both AO1 and AO2 skills. There are also two elements that should be discussed – meaning and purpose. Lower level answers for AO1 will tend just to focus on one of these or deal with both in a very brief manner. It would be expected that answers would cover such things as logical positivism for discussion about meaningful. Good AO2 responses to this area might question the basic assumptions of logical positivism.

The purpose element of the question would include non-cognitive approaches and include such things as evocativeness, giving insight and expressing trust/commitment/worship. The AO2 will be more than descriptive. It will engage in a process of reasoning to present a response to the claim in the question. Higher level AO2 should show awareness of both sides of the debate and reach a justified, appropriate conclusion.

Further questions to consider

1 a) What is meant by language-games?
  b) Why have some scholars claimed that religious language is a language-game?
  c) Evaluate other scholars' arguments for rejecting this claim.

2 'Once we acknowledge the symbolic character of religious language, can we be sure we are talking about anything at all?' Discuss.

BIBLIOGRAPHY

W Alston, *Perceiving God* (Cornell University Press, 1991).

Augustine, *Confessions* (Penguin, 1961).

Augustine, *The City of God* (Penguin, 1972; new edition 1984).

AJ Ayer, *Language, Truth and Logic* (Penguin, 1936).

AJ Ayer, *The Central Questions of Philosophy* (Penguin, 1973).

P Badham, *Immortality or Extinction?* (Macmillan, 1982).

C Blomberg, *The Historical Reliability of the Gospels* (IVP, 1987).

C Brown, *Philosophy and the Christian Faith* (IVP, 1968).

M Buber, *I and Thou* (T&T Clark, 1937).

S Clark, *How to Live Forever* (Routledge, 1995).

AC Clarke, *World of Strange Powers* (Guild, 1985).

W Clifford, *Lectures and Essays* (London, 1879).

P Cole & J Lee, *Religious Language* (Abacus, 1994).

D Cupitt, *Taking Leave of God* (SCM, 1980).

M Curd, *Argument and Analysis: An Introduction to Philosophy* (West Publishing Company, 1992).

A Custance, *The Mysterious Matter of Mind* (Probe Ministries, 1980).

B Davies, *Thinking about God* (Chapman, 1985).

B Davies, *An Introduction to the Philosophy of Religion* (OUP, 1993).

B Davies (ed.), *Philosophy of Religion: A Guide to the Subject* (Cassell, 1998).

C Davis, *The Evidential Force of Religious Experience* (OUP, 1989).

S Davis, *Encountering Evil* (John Knox, 1981).

S Davis, *God, Reason and Theistic Proofs* (Edinburgh University Press, 1997).

F Dostoyevsky, *The Brothers Karamazov* (Penguin, 1958 reprint; first published 1880).

CS Evans, *Thinking about Faith* (IVP, 1985).

N Everitt, *The Non-existence of God* (Routledge, 2003).

P Fenwick, *The Truth in the Light* (Headline, 1995).

A Flew & A MacIntyre (eds), *New Essays in Philosophical Theology* (SCM, 1955).

R Geivett (ed.), *In Defence of Miracles* (IVP, 1997).

J Glover, *The Philosophy and Psychology of Personal Identity* (Penguin, 1988).

B Greyson, Incidence and correlates of near-death experiences on a cardiac care unit (*General Hospital Psychiatry* 25, 2003).

C Hartshorne, *The Logic of Perfection* (La Salle, 1962).

D Hay, *Inner Space* (OUP, 1987).

J Hick, *Evil and the God of Love* (Fontana, 1968).

J Hick, *Arguments for the Existence of God* (Macmillan, 1970).

J Hick, *Death and Eternal Life* (Collins, 1976).

J Hick, *Philosophy of Religion* (Prentice-Hall, 1983).

R Holland, The Miraculous (*American Philosophical Quarterly* 2, 1965).

J Hosper, *An Introduction to Philosophical Analysis* (4th edition) (Routledge, 1997).

D Hume, *Enquiry concerning Human Understanding* (OUP; First published 1777).

D Hume, *Dialogues concerning Natural Religion* (ed. Wilson Pike) (Bobbs-Merrill Educational Publishing, Indiana Press, 1970 reprint).

W James, *The Varieties of Religious Experience* (Penguin, 1902; reprint 1983).

M Johnson, *Philosophical Perspectives on Metaphors* (University of Minnesota Press, 1981).

I Kant, *The Critique of Pure Reason*, trans by N Kemp Smith (St Martin's, 1965).

J Kildahl, *The Psychology of Speaking in Tongues* (Harper & Row, 1972).

CS Lewis, *The Problem of Pain* (Centenary Press, 1940).

CS Lewis, *A Grief Observed* (Faber, 1961).

D MacKay, *The Clockwork Image* (IVP, 1974).

J Mackie, *The Miracle of Theism* (OUP, 1982).

N Malcolm, Anselm's Ontological Arguments (*Philosophical Review* 69, 1960).

F McCutcheon, 'Language Games' (*Dialogue* 7, 1996).

S McFague, *Models of God in Religious Language* (Fortress, 1982).

A McGrath, *Christian Theology: An Introduction* (Blackwell, 1994).

A McKinnon, Miracle and Paradox (*American Philosophical Quarterly* 4, 1967).

R Messer, *Does God's Existence Need Proof?* (Clarendon, 1997).

JS Mill, *Three Essays on Religion* (Longmans Green, 1874).

H Montefiore, *The Probability of God* (SCM, 1985).

R Moody, *Life after Life* (Bantam, 1975).

R Nash, *The Concept of God* (Zondervan Publishing Co., 1983).

J Newman, *Grammar of Assent* (Notre Dame, 1979; first published 1870).

R Otto, *The Idea of the Holy* (OUP, 1917).

HP Owen, *Concepts of Deity* (Macmillan, 1971).

W Paley, *Natural Theology* (Ibis, 1986).

M Palmer, *The Question of God* (Routledge, 2001).

T Penelhum, *Survival and Disembodied Existence* (Routledge, 1970).

W Penfield, *The Physical Basis of Mind* (Blackwell, 1950).

DZ Phillips, *Death and Immortality* (Macmillan, 1971).

A Plantinga, *God, Freedom and Evil* (Eerdmans, 1974).

A Plantinga, *The Nature of Necessity* (OUP, 1974).

K Popper & J Eccles, *The Self and Its Brain* (London, 1977).

H Price, Survival and the Idea of 'Another World' (*Proceedings of the Society for Psychical Research* 50, Part 182, Jan 1953).

J Puddefoot, *God and the Mind Machine* (SPCK, 1996).

I Ramsey, *Religious Language* (SCM, 1957).

J Rhine, *Extrasensory Perception* (Society for Psychical Research, 1934).

J Robinson, *Honest to God* (SCM, 1963).

K Rogers, *Perfect Being Theology* (Edinburgh University Press, 2000).

B Russell, *Why I am not a Christian* (Unwins, 1957).

G Ryle, *The Concept of Mind* (Penguin, 1949).

N Smart, *Philosophers and Religious Truth* (SCM, 1964).

R Solomon, *The Big Questions* (Harcourt Brace, 1998).

J Soskice, *Metaphor and Religious Language* (Clarendon, 1985).

W Stace, *Mysticism and Philosophy* (Macmillan, 1960).

D Stiver, *The Philosophy of Religious Language* (Blackwell, 1996).

St Teresa, *The Collected Works of St Teresa of Avila* (ICS Publications, 1987).

R Swinburne, *The Concept of Miracle* (Macmillan, 1970).

R Swinburne, *The Coherence of Theism* (Clarendon, 1977).

R Swinburne, *The Existence of God* (OUP, 1979).

R Swinburne, *Is There a God?* (OUP, 1996).

FR Tennant, *Philosophical Theology* (CUP, 1930).

A Thiselton, *A Concise Encyclopedia of the Philosophy of Religion* (Oneworld, 2002).

P Tillich, *Systematic Theology* (Nisbet & Co, 1951).

P Tillich, *Dynamics of Faith* (Harper & Bros, 1958).

P Vardy, *The Puzzle of God* (Collins, 1990).

G Vesey & P Foulkes, *Collins Dictionary of Philosophy* (Collins, 1990).

W Wainwright, *Philosophy of Religion* (Wadsworth, 1988).

K Ward, *Holding Fast to God* (Oneworld, 1982).

J Webber, *Faith and Reason* (Abacus, 1995).

J Webber, *Revelation and Religious Experience* (Abacus, 1995).

E Wiesel, *The Trial of God* (Penguin, 1979).

M Wiles, *God's Action in the World* (SCM, 1986).

I Wilson, *The After Death Experience* (Guild, 1987).

L Wittgenstein, *Philosophical Investigations* (Blackwell, 1953).

L Wittgenstein, *Tractatus Logico-Philosophicus* (Routledge, 1961 (1921)).

R Zaehner, *Concordant Discord* (OUP, 1970).

C Zaleski, *Otherworld Journeys* (OUP, 1988).

FURTHER READING

General coverage

B **Magee**, *The Story of Philosophy* (Dorling Kindersley, 1998).
D **Palmer**, *Does the Centre Hold?* (Mayfield, 1996).
M **Peterson**, *Reason and Religious Belief* (OUP, 1991).
M **Peterson**, *Philosophy of Religion: Selected Readings* (OUP, 1996).
M **Oliver**, *Hamlyn History: Philosophy* (Hamlyn, 1997).
M **Thompson**, *Teach Yourself Philosophy of Religion* (Hodder, 1997).

Arguments (Chapter 1)

N **Warburton**, *Thinking from A–Z* (Routledge, 1996).

Nature of God (Chapter 2)

R **Nash**, *The Concept of God* (Zondervan Publishing Co., 1983).
HP **Owen**, *Concepts of Deity* (Macmillan, 1971).
K **Rogers**, *Perfect Being Theology* (Edinburgh University Press, 2000).

Existence of God arguments (Chapters 3–7)

S **Davis**, *God, Reason and Theistic Proofs* (Edinburgh University Press, 1997).
M **Palmer**, *The Question of God* (Routledge, 2001).

Miracles (Chapter 8)

C **Blomberg**, *The Historical Reliability of the Gospels* (IVP, 1987).
N **Cantwell**, *Miracles* (Abacus, 2001).
R **Geivett** (ed.), *In Defence of Miracles* (IVP, 1997).

The value of theistic proofs (Chapter 9)

R **Messer**, *Does God's Existence Need Proof?* (Clarendon, 1997).

Faith and reason (Chapter 10)

J **Webber**, *Faith and Reason* (Abacus, 1995).

Problem of evil (Chapter 11)

S **Davis**, *Encountering Evil* (John Knox, 1981).
J **Hick**, *Evil and the God of Love* (Macmillan reprint, 1991).

Mind and body (Chapter 12)

P **Carruthers**, *Introducing Persons* (Routledge, 1994).

Life after death (Chapter 13)

F **Ma'sumian**, *Life after Death* (Oneworld, 1995).

Religious language (Chapter 14)

B **Magee**, *Confessions of a Philosopher* (Phoenix, 1998).
D **Stiver**, *The Philosophy of Religious Language* (Blackwell, 1996).

On-line resources for this book and others in the series

New books and websites are appearing all the time. Keep up-to-date and share your own suggestions with other students and teachers.

For suggestions for further reading, comments from the authors of the *Access to Religion and Philosophy* series and further advice for students and teachers, **log on to the *Access to Religion and Philosophy* website at:**

www.philosophyandethics.com/access.htm

TIMELINE OF PHILOSOPHERS

470–399BCE	Socrates	1818–1883	Karl Marx
c.428–347BCE	Plato	1838–1900	Henry Sidgwick
384–322BCE	Aristotle	1844–1900	Friedrich Nietzsche
341–270BCE	Epicurus	1871–1947	H. A. Prichard
c.334–262BCE	Zeno	1873–1958	G. E. Moore
50–130CE	Epictetus	1877–1971	W. D. Ross
121–180CE	Emperor Marcus Aurelius	1886–1965	Paul Tillich
1225–1274	Thomas Aquinas	1889–1951	Ludwig Wittgenstein
1588–1679	Thomas Hobbes	1889–1976	Martin Heidegger
1632–1677	Spinoza	1896–1980	Jean Piaget
1632–1704	John Locke	1900–1980	Eric Fromm
1646–1715	Gottfried Leibniz	1905–1980	Jean-Paul Sartre
1671–1713	Earl of Shaftesbury	1905–1991	Joseph Fletcher
1692–1752	Bishop Butler	1908–1979	C. L. Stevenson
1694–1746	Francis Hutcheson	1908–1986	Simone de Beauvoir
1711–1776	David Hume	1910–1989	A. J. Ayer
1712–1778	Jean-Jacques Rousseau	1917–1981	John Mackie
1724–1804	Immanuel Kant	1919–1999	Iris Murdoch
1737–1809	Thomas Paine	1919–2001	Elizabeth Anscombe
1748–1832	Jeremy Bentham	1919–2002	R. M. Hare
1768–1834	Friedrich Schleiermacher	1919–2002	John Rawls
1770–1831	Georg Hegel	1927–1987	Lawrence Kohlberg
1788–1860	Arthur Schopenhauer	1929–2003	Bernard Williams
1801–1890	John Henry Newman	1940–	John Finnis
1806–1873	J. S. Mill	1946–	Peter Singer
1813–1855	Søren Kierkegaard		

GLOSSARY

A contingent being a being, such that if it exists, it cannot not exist.

Agnostic a person who does not believe it is possible to know whether God exists.

Analogy a comparison of two or more things to show how they are similar.

Analytic a statement where the predicate is contained in the subject.

A necessary being a being who is not dependent on any other for its existence.

Anthropic argument nature planning in advance for the needs of humans.

Anti-realism truth is relative to the community who are making the statement.

Anti-realists those who believe a statement is true if it fits in (coheres) with other true statements. Reality is separate from language.

A posteriori from or after experience.

A priori prior to experience.

Argument a set of statements which is such that one of them (the conclusion) is supported or implied by the others (the premises).

Aristotelian relating to Aristotle or his philosophy.

Atheism a belief that there is no God.

Atonement the reconciliation of human beings with God through the sacrificial death of Christ.

Basic belief a belief that is either self-evident, incorrigible (cannot be mistaken) or evident to the senses.

Belief-in a belief that conveys an attitude of trust or commitment.

Belief-that a belief that claims to be an objective fact.

Big Bang theory the theory of an expanding universe that began as an infinitely dense and hot medium at some finite time in the past. The initial instant is called the Big Bang.

Blik a framework within which events are interpreted.

Categorical imperative an imperative such as 'Do x' is categorical when it disregards wishes and desires. For Kant, the categorical imperative was the principle that one should act on a maxim only if one can will that it becomes a universal law.

Category mistake the mistake committed when an object or concept that belongs in one category is treated as if it belongs in a category of a different logical type.

Classical theism traditional Western belief about the nature and attributes of God.

Cognitive statements statements that are true or false in the ways that literal statements are true or false.

Coherency theory this claims that a statement is true if it coheres with other statements.

Contingent that which need not be, that which could have been different; something that has dependency.

Contradictory something that is at variance with itself.

Conversion the changing from one set of beliefs to another.

Correspondence theory of truth this claims that a statement is true if it corresponds to something in the real world.

Cosmology the study of the nature and order of the universe.

Cryptomnesia the memory of the subconscious.

Cultural relativism the acts which are designated right and wrong differ from one culture to another.

Cumulative argument a collection of arguments that together increase the persuasiveness of the case.

Darwinism the theory of natural selection to account for changes in nature.

Deductive argument an argument whose structure dictates that if the premises are true, the conclusion must be true.

Deism the view that God created the universe but is now not directly involved in creation.

Disembodied existence an existence without a body.

Dualism a fundamental twofold distinction, such as mind and body.

Emotivism claiming that an act is right or wrong is expressing an emotion or attitude, not a fact.

Empiricism the view that the dominant foundation of knowledge is experience.

Empiricist one who believes that all knowledge derives from experience.

Enlightenment an eighteenth-century philosophical movement that stressed the importance of reason.

Epiphenomenalism mental events are caused by brain events but are themselves causally impotent.

Epistemic distance a distance from knowledge of God. God is hidden and so this allows human beings to choose freely.

Equivocal the same word is used with a different meaning or is ambiguous.

Eschatological verification the view that some religious ideas are verifiable after death (or at the end of time).

ESP extra-sensory perception.

Ex nihilo Latin phrase meaning 'out of nothing', that is, God did not use any previously existing materials when He created.

Fallacy an error in reasoning.

Falsification principle the theory that sentences are only meaningful if some evidence can count against them.

Fideism the view that certain beliefs are beyond the scope of reason and must be accepted on faith.

Foundational (basic) beliefs a belief that is not derived from any other belief.

Foundationalism the view that beliefs must be supported by evidence or by basic beliefs.

Functionalism expressing the mind and body relationship as descriptions of their causal roles.

Glossolalia speaking in tongues, that is, speaking in an unknown language.

Identity theory the mind and the brain refer to the same object but they have different meanings.

Immanence God's involvement in his creation.

Incarnation God taking on human form in the person of Jesus.

Incoherent lacking in clarity or consistency.

Incorporeal without material form.

Inductive argument an argument whose structure dictates that even if the premises are true, the conclusion may not be true.

Ineffable indescribable, cannot be expressed in words.

Intelligent design the view that an intelligent cause (which is not identified) accounts for certain features of the universe. Its supporters claim that it is a 'scientific' theory.

Irreducible complexity when all parts of a system must be in place in order for the system to work. The removal of any one of the parts causes the system to stop functioning.

Language-games a term used by Wittgenstein to refer to any particular context in which language is used.

Law of nature a generalisation based on regular happenings within nature.

Logical positivists a movement which developed from the Vienna Circle. They sought to find the ultimate test for meaningful statements – the verification principle.

Materialism the view that the material universe is all that exists.

Metaphor a word or phrase is applied to an object that it does not literally denote, in order to convey a resemblance.

Middle knowledge God knows what every creature would do in any given set of circumstances, even if those circumstances never actually occur.

Modal the mode in which something occurs, for example, either necessary or possible.

Model something that represents something else and helps us to understand the original.

Monotheism the belief that there is only one God.

Moral relating to human behaviour and what ought and ought not be done.

Mysticism the experience of having apprehended an ultimate reality.

Myth a symbolic story that tries to explain a fundamental issue about the purpose of existence.

Natural theology the use of reasoned argument to assess basic religious claims, such as the existence of God.

Naturalism an account of the world in terms of natural causes and natural forces.

Near-death experience an out-of-the-body experience occurring at the time of actual or threatened imminent death.

Necessary being a being whose non-existence would be a self-contradiction. This is its sense in the ontological argument. It can also be used in the causal sense, of a being who is required as an explanation.

Neo-Wittgensteinian a new or modern form of Wittgenstein's philosophy.

Noble the quality whereby something is valuable in itself rather than as a means to some other good thing.

Noetic relating to the mind.

Non-cognitive statements statements that are not open to truth or falsity at all.

Numen something that is 'wholly other' than the natural world.

Objective external to the mind, actually existing.

Occam's razor the principle that entities should not be multiplied beyond necessity.

Omnipotent God is able to do all His holy will.

Omniscient God knows all things actual and possible.

Ontological concerned with being.

Oscillating universe theory the theory that there has been an infinite series of expanding and contracting universes.

Pantheism the idea that the whole universe is God or part of God.

Passivity not active, not participating in the activity.

Philosophical behaviourism mental events are really ways of referring to complex patterns of behaviour.

Philosophy literally 'a love of wisdom'. The actual subject area is disputed and ranges from linguistic analysis to questions about ultimate reality.

Planck's constant used in Quantam mechanics to describe the sizes of quanta.

Poltergeist the literal meaning is 'noisy spirit'.

Possible world anything that can be conceived of, or is logically consistent.

Prayer inward communication with the divine.

Predicate the part of a sentence in which something is asserted or denied of the subject.

Privation of good an absence or lack of good. A malfunctioning of something that in itself is good.

Process theology emphasises 'becoming' rather than 'being'. God is not seen as omnipotent but is changeable and persuasive.

Proof a sequence of steps that establishes the truth of a proposition.

Psychokinesis the ability to move objects using the power of the mind.

Qualia felt experiences such as tasting a hamburger.

Realists those who believe that a statement is true if it corresponds to an actual state of affairs.

Reincarnation the transmigration of the soul from body to body.

'Replica' theory the theory that an identical recreation of a person constitutes them being regarded as the same person.

Revealed theology claims about God derived from 'revelations' from special experiences of God or sacred writings.

Scepticism the view that we can know very little, perhaps nothing at all.

Second-order good a moral good that is a response to evil.

Soul-deciding people's response to evil decides their destiny.

Soul-making the presence of evil helps people to grow and develop.

Spiritualism the belief that the dead communicate with the living, through a medium.

Subjective having its source within the mind.

Summum bonum the highest good, which comprises virtue and happiness.

Symbol something that represents something else and evokes participation.

Synthetic a statement where the predicate is not contained in the subject.

Teleological the study of ends or final causes, particularly as evidence for design and purpose in nature.

Telepathy the communicating of mind with mind.

Theism the belief in the existence of God transcendent – having existence outside the universe.

Theistic belief in the existence of one divine reality, who is distinct from creation.

Theodicy a justification of the righteousness of God, given the existence of evil.

Transcendent God is greater than and distinct from his creation.

Transiency not permanent. Lasting for short time only.

Univocal the same word is used with exactly the same meaning.

Valid argument the correct logical structure of a deductive argument.

Verification principle the theory that sentences are only meaningful if they can be verified by the senses.

Via negativa literally, the way of negation – understanding God by saying what He is not.

Zener cards a pack of 25 cards showing five each of several simple symbols: plus sign, star, circle, square and three wavy lines.

INDEX